SUDDENLY

Single

SURVIVING THE DEMISE OF YOUR RELATIONSHIP

Jan Mitchell

© Copyright 2022

IBG Publications, LLC

JAN MITCHELL

Published by I.B.G. Publications, LLC, a Power to Wealth Company

Web Address: WWW.IBGPublications.Com

admin@IBGPublications.Com / 904-419-9810

Copyright, 2022 by Venus Chandler

IBG Publications, LLC, Jacksonville, FL

ISBN 978-1-956266-14-6

Mitchell, Jan
SUDDENLY Single: Surviving the Demise of Your Relationship

All rights reserved. This book or its parts may not be reproduced in any form, stored in a retrieval system, or transmitted in any form, by any means-electronic, mechanical, photocopy, recording or otherwise, without prior written permission of the publisher or author, except as provided by the United States of America Copyright law.

Printed in the United States of America.

SUDDENLY *Single*

Dedication

I am dedicating this book to my children: Maurice, Daurice, Diamond, my grandchildren and their grandchildren, and their grandchildren's grandchildren.

I want you to know and understand that I desired to leave a legacy for you to know my name and understand that I want the best for you! I want you to understand that I have made so many horrible choices in my life but the love that I have for you all was my fuel for change.

I wanted to become a mother and a grandmother who you could be proud to call your own. A Mother and a grandmother who you could be proud to say, "I came from her." I want to live on through your children and grandchildren.

When you read my books, watch my vlogs, you will see me! You will see the good, the bad, the ugly but most of, all you will see the new and improved me! You will see the healed, the whole and the empowered.

Jan Mitchell

Learn from me, my mistakes, bad choices, and all my flaws. I am very transparent and raw so you can be better than I ever was.

I Love you!

Mom/Gana Venus

SUDDENLY *Single*

TABLE OF CONTENTS

DEDICATION... 3

I Should Have Seen It Coming...................... 7
Painful Evidence 45
What Was I Looking For?............................. 75
In Sickness And In Health............................ 87
The Power Of Forgiveness............................ 111
Putting The Pieces Together......................... 119
Because She's "BLAKK"................................ 143

About the Lead Author................................. 169
Meet The Co-Authors.................................... 171

Jan Mitchell

SUDDENLY *Single*

I SHOULD HAVE SEEN IT COMING....

It was the year 2015 and I was yet going through another divorce. Number five to be exact.

I was so embarrassed and never thought in a million years it would have been that way; but it was. It was very real.

Once the divorce was over, I said I would give myself a year before I started looking for love again. I refused to give up on love. If I gave up, I felt like I was giving him control over my heart.

I didn't think I would get married again because at five times and counting, I was running neck and neck with Elizabeth Taylor.

I know a lot of you youngins have no clue who she is but let's just say she was a legend and she had been married eight times to seven different men.

Jan Mitchell

Elizabeth Rosemond Taylor was considered one of the last major stars to have come out of what is known as the old Hollywood studio system. She was known internationally for her beauty, especially for her violet eyes, with which she captured audiences early on in her youth and kept the world hooked.
-www.imdb.com.

* * *

I was coming along pretty good. I was living my life, helping my daughter get through nursing school, spending a lot of time with my grandchildren, and really working on me!

My daughter finally finished nursing school and I could not have been prouder. I helped her gain employment, purchase a car, and move into an apartment for her and her kids. I decided it was time for a change, so I moved into a newly remodeled apartment.

I began exploring more opportunities and life was going great for me. I began studying life coaching skills, started public speaking, was about to release my first book and had launched my first organization. I believed I was on my way and thought my life was truly heading in the right direction. I really believed I was completely healed from my previous marriage.

SUDDENLY *Single*

In 2017, I thought it was time to start looking for love, so I set up an online profile on a dating website. I told myself, "I'll describe EXACTLY what I wanted in a man and not hold back: not one bit!"

I can remember my bio's description: He must love to travel, be spontaneous, goal oriented, no children/child support issues, NOT A SMOKER and he must make at least $75,000 or more per year.

I was very specific because I wanted someone who could match me in every area of life, especially financially.

You see, all my relationships, except for one, I always ended up being the bread winner. This left me taking care of, yeah, you guessed it: the man.

I would usually make more money and I vowed that I didn't want this type of relationship anymore. In my experiences, men who made less money and could not afford to give the things he wished, I would eventually emasculate them. This is why I felt the need to be very clear, honest, and open in my dating profile about what I wanted in a man.

As time went along, I was getting sick and tired of dating online because everyone who I came across was just fake! No one told the truth and most of the men I communicated with wanted sex and that was not happening for me.

One day I decided to hell with it, I'm about to delete this account because I was over it! Just as I was about to delete, I said to myself, "Let me take a look at the messages and see what's there."

As I was scrolling through, I was getting very frustrated and decided to hit the delete account button. That's when his name caught my eye... Let's just call him 'little man.'

I read 'little man's' message and it said, "Hi my name is little man. Here's my number and if you're interested, please call me."

I thought to myself hmmmm... interesting. All the other men always asked for my number and never offered theirs. I took 'little man's' number and put it up just in case I changed my mind and wanted to call him later.

A few weeks after taking down little man's number, I began preparing for my trip to Aruba where I'd be gone for two weeks. I started thinking more about calling 'little man.'

SUDDENLY *Single*

One day I picked up the phone and called him and we talked until the wee hours of the morning.

We talked about everything.

He asked to take me out, but I told him that I was leaving for Aruba and it would have to wait until I returned home. I told him I would call him while I was in Aruba whenever I could find the time. He agreed and expressed that he couldn't wait to see me.

I ended up going to Aruba and had an amazing time! I met a pilot while I was there, and we went out for dinner. I could barely give the pilot my energy and attention because I had 'little man' on the brain.

Why couldn't I stop thinking about, 'little man?'

I ended up leaving that date and headed to my hotel room so I could call little man. The phone rang and rang, but no answer. At the time, I was so upset but I didn't feel I had the right to be, so I let it go. Little did I know; this was the first of many red flags to come.

I awoke the next day with little man still on my mind. Although I was breaking all my rules, I said, "The heck with it, I'm going to call him once again just to see if he will answer."

Jan Mitchell

I called and was very surprised he answered. I told him I called the night before and he said he was asleep and did not hear the phone. We spoke on the phone for a while, and he told me to call him the next evening. I called him, but again he did not answer. I was pissed and promised myself that I was completely done with 'little man' and was never going to speak to him again.

The next day came around and I was sad because I was sick of the games men play and was over it. That's when the phone rang....

Half drunk, I looked at my phone and answered with a major attitude. He fed me the same lie that he was asleep and how sorry he was because he did not hear the phone ring. But the anger in me rose, and I was like, "EFF that!"

I told him he didn't have to play games and if he was not interested, he didn't need to call me anymore; it was no sweat off my back.

Little man said, "I promise, I'm not playing games; I work a really hard job and when I lie down, I can drift into a deep sleep."

SUDDENLY *Single*

After some convincing, which didn't take much, I gave in and said "OK."

With all his charm, he said, "I can't wait to see you when you return so I can take you on a date."

For the remainder of the day and night, I was on cloud nine and couldn't wait to get back to Los Angeles.

As soon as I went through customs leaving Aruba, I called little man to let him know I was on my way back to Los Angeles. Once again, he did not answer the phone, so, I decided to call him on my layover.

I called little man on my layover, and he still did not answer my call. I was so upset and didn't really know what to do at that point. When I think back, I was teaching him how to treat me. I was teaching him that this behavior was ok.

Suddenly Single Moment
-A man learns how to treat you from your signs of self-love or hatred.

— Coach Venus

JAN MITCHELL

I arrived in Los Angeles and called little man one more time. I told myself if he didn't answer, I would ditch his number. I called and **still** no answer.

I was in such disbelief because we had such good chemistry over the phone, and I really thought he was the one. The main reason I felt like he was the one was because I was comfortable with his conversation. We had not met in person, but I sensed a genuine connection.

Believe it or not, that's a red flag as well. Anytime someone feels familiar to you, pay close attention to **why!** Usually, it's because you are familiar with this type of person based on a previous experience with the same *type* of person. As humans, we tend to steer toward what is comfortable for us, even if it's unhealthy.

I arrived home and started unpacking my clothes and began wondering how did it all go wrong? What had I done wrong or said wrong? Was I lacking what 'little man' wanted or *any* man?

As my mind was in this whirlwind of 'why,' the phone rang. I looked at the phone, and there he was calling, 'little man.'

SUDDENLY *Single*

I hesitated for a minute; but **why** was I willing to entertain his lie? He told me he had to get a new phone, and this delayed his call. In my mind, body, and soul I knew it was a lie. But even after all I had been through in my previous marriages, I ignored **all** the red flags. They were not just waving at me but thrown in my face about this man.

'Little man' asked if he could take me out and I said, "Yes." We decided we would go to the beach and have drinks on the upcoming Saturday. As a joke, I told little man if he was ugly in person I would go on the date with him, drink and eat up all his money and catch an uber home.

We laughed and he said, "I'm pretty sure that won't happen."

Saturday came and I was nervous as all get out. I decided to wear a nice pair of jean shorts, an off the shoulders top and a pair of sandals; I always thought my feet were my best assets.

Little man arrived and I was praying to God he was not ugly in person. Funny, how that meant more to me than all those d%@!* red flags.

Little man pulled up and my eyes lit all the way up.

Jan Mitchell

He was a little smaller than what I anticipated but he was sexy as hell! He was bald with a white go tee, bow legged and red bone complexion.

He wore wire frame glasses, which was ok by me because it made him look more important, smarter, and sexier. I invited little man upstairs to meet my daughter since I was going to be riding in his car. I felt like it was good she met him because she was a very good judge of character in men and would speak the truth.

We went to Venice Beach to my favorite restaurant, "The Waterfront Café." This restaurant always seemed so magical to me. Everyone who came there always appeared to be so happy and carefree. The restaurant sat in a perfect spot where you could look straight out to at the ocean, and the breeze was everything; especially when you are with great company.

Little man and I talked about everything, and it felt as though I had found the one who I wanted to spend the rest of my life with. I felt so comfortable with him that I shared my shame with him: shame he later used against me. I looked him in the eye and said, "Little man, there is something I need to tell you and you may not want to date me anymore."

SUDDENLY *Single*

He looked at me and said, "I'm sure there is nothing you can tell me that would make me run."

Believe it or not, this was *another* hint.

I looked him in the eyes and said, "I've been married five times and I just got a divorce about a year ago."

He said, "Whew, I thought you were going to tell me something bad." He then said to me, "Well, I have a secret too." He went on, "I've been to prison before."

I never asked him why, when, how or anything. I just accepted it because I thought, "Girl, you all used up, who are you to be judging anyone?"

Our date went amazing and from that day forward, we were inseparable.

* * *

The next day, my daughter told me that little man was a bum who was looking for a woman with money and somewhere to live. I thought my daughter was jealous because I was falling for this man and my time and attention was on him and not on her.

That's another rule lol. 😊

Pay close attention to your family and friends when they see something in a man or woman you don't see. When your hormones are raging and you are in the moment, there are things you will not see and brush off.

> **Suddenly Single Moment**
> -Listen to your family and friends who see things you do not see in a potential mate.
>
> —Coach Jenny

Shortly after my daughter shared her opinion, we ended up getting into a big falling out. Instead of little man trying to make it better, he made sure that my daughter and I split. This was another clue I totally overlooked.

Why would anyone want to see a mother and daughter bump heads and not speak? It seems like if he meant any good, he would attempt to be the peace maker and not add fuel to the fire, right? This was the beginning of my isolation, and I did not see it coming.

We had been dating for months, yes months when we decided to shack up. I felt nothing was wrong with it because we were two consensual adults who could do what they wanted.

Yes, I allowed a stranger to move into my home. The few short months that we were dating was nowhere near enough time to allow someone to come in and live in your space. I knew this was not right, but I did not want to hear anyone's opinion about it, especially my kids.

So secretly, I moved him in.

Little man treated me like a queen. He was buying me things, taking me out and hell, he even took me on a romantic dinner cruise. No other man had ever been as good to me as little man was in the beginning of our relationship. Yes, I say beginning because it started going downhill quickly but I refused to see all the red flags waving around and banging me across the head.

I remember coming home from work excited that I was going to see little man. As I was walking up to the apartment door, I got a call from a man who wanted to interview me for a newspaper out of Akron, Ohio. He wanted to discuss my book titled, "A Silent Scream, My Story, My Truth."

I walked into the house talking with the journalist over

the phone and when I got off, little man lit into me.

He said, "You must think I'm a fool. You are talking on the phone with some dude while I'm right here."

I was so confused. When I tried to explain myself, he was not hearing it. He gave me the silent treatment for three days. It was the craziest three days of my life.

Once my book released, I caught back lash from my family, and my aunt and I were no longer speaking. All of this made me feel alone. With little man not speaking to me, I felt alone and as though there was no one to turn to, not even the person I shared my personal space with. This should have been one of the biggest red flags, but I still chose to ignore it.

Three days later we began speaking again. It was very uncomfortable and there were no apologies of any sort. I still was very confused and did not understand what happened. As usual I swept it under the rug and taught little man how to treat me.

Months later, little man said he wanted to move and had found a house in Covina, CA. This was about an hour and fifteen minutes from LA, placing distance between the little bit of family and friends I had in the area.

Nevertheless, I went and looked at the house along with my two best friends and I loved it immediately. A couple weeks later we were moving in.

What I overlooked during this time is little man put no money towards this move. I did not question it at the time, and I don't really know why.

I ended up paying for the entire move including furnishing the entire house! This was also another way he succeeded at isolating me from all my friends and family.

> **Suddenly Single Moment**
> -A man who does not contribute monetarily is a man who may become financially abusive.
>
> —Coach Jenny

* * *

During the first few months of our new move, I began learning things about little man. I found out he had no credit, made **little** money, and owed child support out the a@!!

Instead of running for the hills, I supported him like any good woman would. I helped him build his credit, started a new business so he could have additional money and could live after paying all his child support.

You know? Trying to be that down a@! chic. Ladies if you are not down for yourself, then you can never be down for anyone else!

The first credit card he was able to get had an eleven-thousand-dollar credit line along with some others. I thought we were on our way, and he appreciated my efforts to improve his lifestyle. Little did I know, he **despised** me for it. It seemed like the more I tried to help build him up, the more he despised me.

Even after all my efforts to make our relationship work, things started going downhill fast. Little man became really mean with me, talking to me like I was a piece of trash and saying things to belittle me.

I was so confused, sad, and hurt. Especially since I was not speaking to my aunt or daughter. I had no one else to talk to so I went and talked to his sister who was not surprised at all. In fact, every time we attended family functions, the family would say, maybe little man changed; maybe he isn't who he used to be.

SUDDENLY *Single*

I continued ignoring all the signs, never questioned why his family said these things about him. Through all of this, I remained in the relationship.

* * *

As time went by, little man became meaner, the laughter stopped, the compliments ceased, and even the friendship came to an end. Little man didn't even come inside the house until it was time for him to go to bed. He even stopped having sex with me. When I asked for it, he would act like it was a chore.

After we got married, he lied and said he was having older men's problems. Basically, he lied and said that his penis wasn't working. I started thinking I was not good enough, ugly, and not worthy. I still didn't understand what I had done wrong. I couldn't see this was narcissism at it best.

Narcissists use some of these tactics to remain in control and it helps them feel superior, making you inferior. They make you feel like you're the blame, or crazy; they make **you** the one with the problem.

When I felt like this man hated me and sure he did not want to be with me anymore, he would make me feel appreciated by taking me to his mother's house for fish and shrimp. It caught me off guard because it was a Friday and we never went to his mom's house on a weekday, only on weekends. If it meant us being together, it was ok by me.

We arrived at his mother's house, and it was a lot of his family there. I wondered why everyone was there but just brushed it off.

We ate and talked a bit when suddenly little man said, "Why aren't we married yet?"

I said, "I don't know, you have never asked me," and attempted to walk away.

Little man pulled me back close to him and when I turned around, he got down on one knee and asked me to marry him. I was in such shock because of the way he had been treating me. I immediately said, "Yes," and assumed it would get better from there.

I was on cloud nine after that amazing proposal! I thought we had ventured into new beginnings, but h

I was on cloud nine after that amazing proposal! I thought we had ventured into new beginnings, but how wrong I was.

We, (I) immediately started planning the wedding.

SUDDENLY *Single*

Since there was a lot of his family coming into Vegas, we (I) decided we would get married there and little man agreed.

We continued planning, but things between us kept getting worse. He kept talking to me like I was nothing and belittling me. As I was shopping for my wedding dress, I realized that I had put on a lot of weight in such a short period of time. When this happens, it's usually because I'm depressed and unhappy. I still chose to ignore all the signs and move forward with the wedding.

I knew early in the game that little man was not the man for me. But I was so ashamed, I felt "Who would want me?" I was on my sixth marriage and felt like if he sees how good I am to him, he will return to treating me good.

* * *

The weekend before we got married little man and a couple of his friends went out for a night out on the town. I allowed him to take my Camaro SS so that he would look the part. You know, fit in with his friends?

Around 3:00 AM, I noticed he hadn't returned home. I waited and waited when finally, I called his mom.

JAN MITCHELL

His mother called little man's friends, but no one had heard from him.

Finally, I received a call from little man at 7:00 AM. I asked where he was and he stated, "I'm in jail, please come get me."

I asked where he was located and he said, "San Diego."

I was so bewildered, and I asked how, why, what happened? He started getting smart with me on the phone and he talked to me so badly, I hung up on him.

Little man called back and said, "I'm sorry please just come get me."

I asked where my car was, and he said it was impounded. I just hung up the phone and called his sister for a ride.

We drove to San Diego, I cried the entire time and said I was not marrying this man. Why did I choose to ignore those red flags that were being thrown at my head? All I knew was that I loved this man, or should I say, I loved his representative?

SUDDENLY *Single*

> **Suddenly Single Moment**
> -A narcissist will never show up in a relationship as their true self. They always send a representative: the person they desire you to see.
> —*Coach Venus*

* * *

After retrieving my car from the impound, I noticed women's items were in my car and it took me for a loop. I was so pissed off yet hoping he had not been out with someone else.

Eight hundred dollars later, between bailing him out of jail, and getting my car out of tow we were on our way home. There was never an 'I'm sorry, I'll do better, or it's all a misunderstanding.' Nothing.

I asked about the items that were in my car and he stated that they were his cousins' friends' items. I knew that was a lie but did not have proof. The fact remained: I did not want to believe the truth.

The following week we got married as planned November 24, 2018, in a small wedding chapel in Las Vegas, Nevada. A lot of his family were there, but only my baby daughter and two best friends were there for me.

I knew I had no business marrying this man. He was not there for me emotionally, physically, financially and he did not support any of my endeavors. I knew at this point little man did not really want to marry me and he had already cheated on me. I refused to acknowledge the red flags thrown at my head and I was too embarrassed to call off the wedding.

After getting married, for some reason I thought things would get better, but over time, things got worse.

One day after coming back from one of his family functions in Tennessee we got into a bad argument because he disrespected his gay niece in public whose feelings were hurt.

While in our room at the Air BNB, after the incident, I told him he hurt her bad. His response was, "I don't give a f*#!"
I said to him, "How can you be so cold?"

Suddenly, he exchanged his rage for her towards me and began calling me names and making accusations that I was gay.

SUDDENLY *Single*

Once we arrived home, he got in my face screaming and calling me names. When he called me a b*!#$, I lost my breath and I realized things would never be the same.

Little man was so irate he swung at me, snatching my phone out of my hand, and throwing it to the ground. I took a deep breath, picked up my phone and gathered some clothes to leave. He started crying and begged me not to go expressing he was very sorry. This should have been another clue; I should have left and never looked back.

After the Tennessee incident things were never the same. The business I helped him to start he forced me out of and became very secretive about the money and moves he was making. I found out he took out two loans and never told me about it.

The reason I found out is because one morning he came running in the house stating someone broke into his car and took ten thousand dollars from his glove compartment.

I was blown away.

When I asked where he got it from, he never answered but said, "Oh, it was supposed to be a surprise for you."

Jan Mitchell

I knew it was a lie because he never offered to pay the bills the whole three months I had been off from work with a broken ankle.

One day I finally realized that I was paying all the bills in the house and all his money was benefiting him and him only.

We were preparing to buy a house and I knew we could get what we wanted because we both had great credit: so, I thought.

When the realtor called me and said little man's credit was not good enough and all his credit cards were maxed out, I hit the roof. I called up little man and told him what the realtor said and that's when little man let me have it.

He said, "How the f*#! am I supposed to live? I don't have any money!"

I raised an eyebrow. At that moment, I told myself it was time to wake up and find out who I was married to. I should have done this long before I committed to him in a relationship, let alone marriage.

I ended up overhearing a conversation with him and the child support agency. I learned that he owed over one hundred thousand dollars for just **one** child who was now in her 30's but was not his biological child. After finding that out I also learned that he owed back child support for two others and current support on his youngest child. This was the reason he did not have any money: they were taking over half of his paycheck.

After learning about his child support woes, I started doing some digging. I found out that he had a long criminal record and had been in prison multiple times for horrible crimes. I also learned that he was gang affiliated and there were people who wanted to take him out.

I started paying closer attention to what was going on around the house and took note that little man was spending all his time in the garage. He would come in the house to eat and go to bed, but the intimacy was completely gone. There was no sex, hugs, kisses, touching, gazing at me in a sexy way or nothing. Our relationship was completely dead!

I noticed he was babysitting his phone more and keeping it on vibrate. We tried counseling but little man continued to act like I was the problem, and he just did not want to be with me anymore.

Jan Mitchell

* * *

My foster mom ended up getting sick and was told that she had a very short time to live. I was flying back and forth between Ohio and California. Every time I was in Ohio, I noticed he was never at home, would not call and check on me and half the time, he would not answer his phone. I knew then more than ever before that little man was cheating and our marriage was over.

One time when I arrived back from Ohio, and while I was there, he accused me of cheating. I knew he was accusing me because this was what **he** was doing.

Our marriage became worser with little man calling me names, sleeping on the couch, and belittling me. He even said to me, "That's what's wrong with you black women, yawl talk too damn much!" I was so insulted, and I was done at that moment.

On Thanksgiving Day, we were sitting on the sectional couch at opposite ends from one another. I was drifting in and out of sleep, but I caught a glimpse of him looking at his phone and then sitting it down. He would pick it up, look at it, look over his shoulder at me and then text something.

I was pretending to be sleep but then I said to myself the next time he picks up that phone, I'm picking up mine. When he picked his phone up, I picked mine up and when I got the chance, I took a picture of his messages and saved them.

Yes, he was talking to some chick. A little while later, he picked a fight with me and got dressed and left. I waited for about thirty minutes and called him. I said I did not realize that he was going somewhere and leaving me at home on the holiday. He told me he just needed to get away from me and needed some time by himself. At that moment on that day, I started plotting my exit!

> **Suddenly Single Moment**
> -Remember? I told you when you meet a man, you teach him how to treat you. This behavior was ok because I tolerated it from the start.
> —*Coach Venus*

* * *

I started moving things of importance out of the house little by little and packed up all my belongings. He never asked questions but mentioned to me that this was so embarrassing.

I made sure I got important documents and took

pictures of his ID, birth certificate, and pay stubs. I also made sure to put bleach in his artificial urine that he used to beat drug tests at work.

December came and I was ready to make my move! I prepared the U-Haul and movers the day before and when little man left for work, me and the movers got busy and moved everything out of the house that was mine. I also made sure I took all the equipment I bought prior to marriage because I wasn't leaving anything for him to benefit from. Anything else I did not want I trashed and cut up any furniture left behind. I destroyed the bed with a sledgehammer because I refused to lie in that bed every again!

And with that, I was **'SUDDENLY Single!'**

I was homeless but happy and relieved I was free from little man. But then the phone calls of threats to beat my a*#, or have someone else to beat my a*#.

His threats became real and started happening when he showed up at my job. At first, I was afraid because little man is a dangerous person and I believed what he was telling me. I had no choice but to let my job know and then I filed a restraining order. Once I did that, I went and purchased a gun, a nine-millimeter to be exact. I was trained to use it and would have if necessary.

I did extend a courtesy to his mother by calling to put her on notice that if her son attempted to harm me in anyway, I will defend myself without hesitation.

* * *

I temporarily moved in with my youngest daughter and her boyfriend. When I tell you, I was so embarrassed! I was at my lowest and saw myself as a complete failure: this was an understatement.

I cried every night, asking God, "What did I do wrong?"

I began working myself to death almost daily. I was attempting to run away from the pain and didn't have anywhere to run to. I tried hard to fake it for everyone and make it seem as though I was ok, but I was far from ok.

I was dying inside, and I did not know what to do or which way to turn. I knew I needed a therapist to sort this stuff out, but I just wanted to die! I really thought this was the man, I thought we were best friends, I thought I was being a "good wife."

My heart hurt every day and even after all he had done to me, I still loved him and that made me sick to my stomach.

I had horrible thoughts about bringing harm to him by flattening his tires, putting sugar in his tank, or calling his job and getting him fired. I thought of so many things I could do to hurt him but the God in me would not allow me.

I kept hearing God say, "Continue to pray for him and the woman he cheated with. Wish him well, that's where your healing lies."

I was so mad at God because I wanted to wish death on him **and** the female.

* * *

After living with my daughter for about four months I decided it was time that I face living alone: I went and got my own place.

My new place was like a vacation resort. It has pools, Jacuzzis and all the amenities that one could dream of. After moving into my own place, it was time to start my journey to healing.

SUDDENLY *Single*

The first thing I did was file for a divorce so that I could put the marriage behind me, and that piece of the process would be done.

After filing for my divorce, I cried for almost a year, I was very angry and couldn't understand.

I told God, "I don't understand. Why would someone want to cheat with him? He had nothing. I helped build him up, I was there when he was struggling and had nothing."

At that moment I decided to call him the little bitty b!*# boy with the teeny tiny dick! I was pissed off that this non dick having, little bitty, broke a*#, in debt a*# man cheated on me.

There, I said it!

* * *

Within that year, I decided to focus only on myself. No men, no dating, not entertaining any men. I knew that I really needed to truly heal this time so that maybe one day I could have healthier relationships.

I was still very angry with my marriage ending SUDDENLY and I still wanted someone to pay. But as I focused more on myself, my anger seemed to disappear little by little.

The first thing I did was confess my truth to all who knew me, virtually and personally. It took everyone for a loop, but I felt it was my duty especially because I am a Life Coach. I never want anyone thinking I have it all together just because I am a Life Coach. I am human, I cry, I get mad, I make mistakes and I'm far from perfect!

Then I decided to buy myself a Harley because I had always wanted one. Up until that point, I had always put others before myself and I never had the extra money to buy one.

I ended up buying a 2018 Street Glide Harley and shortly after, I joined a sisterhood: a motorcycle club. That is where I found my fit.

Riding my Harley and fellowshipping with my club sisters was my therapy. When I am on my bike or with them, I feel free, I feel a sense of belonging and I finally feel like my life is about me.

I then decided to completely reinvent myself by first losing weight. With little man I had got up to a whopping two hundred and thirty-one pounds.

SUDDENLY *Single*

Most people said they didn't notice the weight, but I did. I was able to hide it well since I'm tall.

Being overweight I did not feel confident, or sexy and little man made me feel like I was unattractive and unwanted. I ended up going from two hundred and thirty-one pounds to one hundred and eighty pounds, and I feel AMAZING!

I decided to go one step further and do something I always wanted to do for myself and that was get a tummy tuck and liposuction.

After my surgery, now with a flat belly, curvy body, and my dramatic weight loss, I feel wonderful. All of this did not mean that I was healed, I still had to fix the inside: but this was a great beginning.

Today I am confident, happy, and healthy but still not whole. I have a lot of work to do on myself because the goal is for me to be whole so that when or **if** the time comes, I can be there completely for that special person.

For now, dating is off the table and marriage for me is completely off the table and not an option. This is my decision. Not because I'm scorned but because I love my life as a single person. All the reasons I felt I needed to be married were found to be untrue. Will that ever change? I'm not sure. but I do know that I want no part of it at this point in my life.

Becoming SUDDENLY single changed my life for the better and made me take a very long look in the mirror. I had to stop blaming all those men, they were not at fault. They just played their part. It was **my** job to find out who these men were and look beyond their representative.

I should have made sure I exposed him to more people, especially family and friends. I should have taken note when my daughter who loves me said he was not good enough for me and he was a bum. I later found out he was living in his car when he met me and showering at the gym.

* * *

One of the main things I learned in all of this is to own my own sh!@* and place the blame where it belonged: on me!

Suddenly Single Moment
-All the family and friends who paid attention to the red flags, return to them, and apologize. Thank them for caring enough to tell you the truth.

Coach Jenny

SUDDENLY *Single*

I should not have rushed and did my homework. I should have valued myself more and been my **own** best friend!

When I look back on why I chose the men I did, I feel I chose them because they were safe. Since I had more than what they did, I wouldn't not run the risk of rejection, the furthest thing from the truth.

The men I chose had everything to do with my childhood and the trauma I suffered. I didn't realize it at the time, but this is something I learned specifically during this healing process.

One other thing I learned: not all those men were wrong, and they were not all bad. I had to take a close look at myself because I was the common denominator.

I was the problem, not them. I allowed these men in my life, and they were just being who they were. It was me who tried to change them into who I wanted them to be. It was me who was living in these fantasies. I thought if I dress them up, get them a job and help them become successful, somehow, they would love me.

All untruths!

Another personal truth I realized during this healing process: I was buying love. These men never loved me, they loved what I presented and what I did for them. I never required any of them to work for anything, I gave everything up for free.

> **Suddenly Single Moment**
> -Anything worth having is worth paying for. This healing process taught me my worth:
> I am worth the price.
> —Coach Jenny

This journey of SUDDENLY singleness helped me to grow because I had to tell the raw truth to myself to heal and become whole!

Not to mention, I am a life coach and I want to be able to coach women from a place of healthiness and wholeness. I needed to be real and raw with myself because I require it from my coachees.

Today, I not only love myself, I'm **in love** with me. I am now able to be alone with me because of the love I now have for self. It is my job to protect my heart, space, and peace. This is my job because no one else will do it for me.

SUDDENLY *Single*

Life is so much more beautiful when you live fully in your truth and love yourself first. Take care of your heart, guard your space and peace!

If you are SUDDENLY single for any reason, use this time to take a long look in the mirror and own your stuff. This is your time to reflect on your next chapter but first you must become happy, healthy, and whole.

Don't let anyone rush your process. Take all the time you need even if it takes multiple seasons.

XXOOXX

Venus

JAN MITCHELL

"Don't let the darkness of your past block the light of joy in your present.

WHAT HAPPENED IS DONE!

Stop giving time to things that no longer exist when there is so much joy to be found in the here and now."

~Oprah Winfrey

PAINFUL EVIDENCE

Busy, Busy, Busy...

I had just gotten off work and was on my way to my next gig. I worked fourteen-hour days Monday through Thursday and every Saturday six to eight hours facilitating a domestic violence class.

It didn't seem like much to me because I absolutely loved what I was doing: assisting women affected by abuse.

I instructed court ordered anger management classes, parenting classes and as mentioned on Saturday's domestic violence classes. I loved doing this work because I could relate to these women. I had also been in abusive relationships that resulted in my children being temporarily detained. I felt what better way to give back than to help women who struggle like I did.

JAN MITCHELL

I grew very close to the women I served. We built strong bonds, shared deep secrets and we trusted and protected each other.

On this day, I entered the small classroom with my purse draped across my body and my handouts for my lesson in hand. Occasionally I would run late for class if I ended up leaving late from my regular nine to five job, but I never missed class. I couldn't, these ladies were counting on me to make sure they had their lessons completed by their next court date. If they needed a progress letter to provide to their social worker, I was a crucial part in them getting their children back or their cases closed. There was no way I wanted to be the reason for delaying that process.

Some of the ladies called the center and especially our tiny classroom their COCOON. This was where change took place and they gradually blossomed into these beautiful powerful butterflies.

Usually when I came in class the ladies would be upbeat, sharing food or talking about their cases. The room would be full of energy and these women who initially were distant and ashamed of their reasons for being there had now became close with each other and helped each other. That warmed my heart.

Today though, the energy in the room was different. They were quiet, some were whispering and looked upset. Some even looked like they were crying. The only thing you could hear was the old air conditioning unit that was struggling to keep the tiny classroom cool. Today it seemed louder than usual.

"Ms. Adrianne??" One of the young ladies said, looking up with these eyes clearly trying to hold back tears. It was Cherrelle who was one of the outgoing stronger girls in the group. She shared so openly, and the others gravitated to her.

"Can I talk to you in your office?" Cherelle asked.

"Girl, we are getting a late start, talk to me after class please." I said to her in my playful way. I could tell she was very serious, and she really needed to talk to me.

Her facial expression never changed and by now her tears were falling. I told one of the other young ladies to pass out the hand outs and instruct everyone to start taking turns reading.

"I'll be right back ladies. Please start reading over the handout." I yelled into the classroom.

I grabbed Cherrelle by her hand and walked her down the tiny narrow hallway to my office. We cried often in these classes and this class was my parenting girls. We would have deep conversations that would get emotional, but this was different. I did not know what to expect, this was weird.

Jan Mitchell

Remember we shared a lot in these classes, so they knew a lot about me, and I knew a whole lot about them

"Ms. Adrianne, I have something horrible to tell you." As she wiped tears from her face. She paused a long time.

"Cherrelle, what is it?" Now I am getting scared. I braced myself for what she was going to say. All sorts of stuff started going through my head.

"Ms. Adrianne, I have something to show you." She pulled her cell phone from her back pocket and began scrolling through her photos. She slowly turned her phone towards me.

"Look at this and tell me if you know who this is." She turned the phone towards me, her hands shaking.

I looked at the picture she placed before me. I grabbed the readers/glasses off my desk to get a better Look and pulled the phone closer to me. I had to be seeing wrong. It looked like my boyfriend of 18 years sitting on a bench hugged up with a woman. I re focused and looked at the picture for what seemed to be ten minutes.

I let out a huge sigh. My throat hurt because I was holding back tears. I had to be strong. I had to use this

SUDDENLY *Single*

embarrassing situation as a lesson to my girls, my little sisters as I often referred to
them.

I looked at Cherrelle with the strongest face I could put on and I chuckled and said, "Wow... I guess he likes ugly wig wearing heffas!" with that, I broke out in laughter so hard, so fake, so hurt.

Cherrelle knew I was hurting, she reached over and hugged me. I wanted to break down. I wanted to cry but I couldn't, I had to be strong.

Cherrelle explained to me that her and some of the other girls had been hiking up in Little Rock Creek a popular hiking area in the Antelope Valley. They all recognized Bert, my boyfriend immediately and saw him with this lady who they knew was not me. She said they all decided not to call me but wait and tell me face to face.

She said they had discussed while they were there, they would confront him and the lady. But then they remembered my lessons of "picking your battles" and "avoiding potential hostile confrontation" and collectively decided to wait. She said they were all angry and sad.

I thanked her and insisted we get back in class, but before we left my office, I asked Cherrelle did everyone know? She told me yes. I swallowed hard, gave Cherrelle a hug and headed to the classroom.

"Hey ladies..." I said as I stood in the doorway looking at their sad faces. I loved them.

At that moment I felt the connection of a sisterhood I've always wanted to experience with a group of women, it just happened to be with my parent class, my survivor sisters. My students showed me they had my back and I appreciated that. The classroom had an awkward energy but a loving powerful atmosphere.

> **Suddenly Single Moment**
> -When you get bad news, it's great to have a good support system. In that moment, I realized my nurturing environment had returned to me.
> —Adrianne

"We love you Ms. Adrianne," one of the ladies shouted.

"I love you too" I responded, "Now lets' read our lesson ladies."

My insides shook, my throat ached from holding in

my emotions and my leg was shaking uncontrollably. I was angry, I was sad, but I insisted we complete class. I did not let anyone leave early.

Everyone wanted to hug me once I dismissed class. They made me promise I would not call or deal with it until I arrived home. Lord knows I tried but the minute I packed up and made sure all the ladies were all picked up or off safely on their way home. I climbed in my truck and called home.

* * *

Bert and I had a routine that he would wait until I arrived home so we could eat dinner together. I always looked forward to this time. We discussed our day and shared funny things that happened. We discussed bills and shared information about our mothers and kids.

Tonight, I was running a little behind my normal time but just off by about fifteen to twenty minutes. I called him to let him know I was on my way..

"Hey, I'm on my way...how was your day?" I said

"It was good, you almost here? I'm hungry," he explained.

"I'm probably about ten minutes away. I proceeded to ask him, "Hey were you at Little Rock Creek on Sunday?"

He became silent to the point I had to call out his name a few times. He finally answered. "No, and why?"

I told him someone told me they saw him there. He stuck to his lie, that he was not there. Boy, was he going to be in for a huge surprise when he realized I had a picture, several pictures of him and the woman he was with.

When I walked in the house, he was in his usual spot at the kitchen table. Only this time he could not look me in the face. Every time I looked at him, he looked away.

I told him I had a picture I wanted him to see. His face turned red, I mean really red. I pulled out my phone which housed the pictures Cherrelle had sent me. I handed him my phone and watched his body language. His leg shook, his eyes twitched, and he kept moving uncontrollably and his cheeks got redder and redder.

"So...is it you? Those are your shorts." I asked sarcastically.

His lips quivering, he said, "Nope that's not me." The nervousness he was experiencing caused his voice to crack.

SUDDENLY *Single*

This mutha%$@# was really gonna sit here and say this wasn't him? Are you kidding me? I took a deep breath washed my hands and began to fix our plates for dinner. I heated the food in the microwave and when the bell rang after the two minutes, it was also like a bell went off in my head...

THIS S*#! IS OVER!!!!

I remained silent as I calmly sat his plate in front of him. Lasagna and salad were normally one of our favorites but we both barely touched our food.

He sat there beet red with what I guess was shame and guilt. The only thing you could hear was the TV and the clatter from our utensils hitting the plates. Finally, my anger got the best of me, I could no longer be silent.

"You are a lying muthf*#!" I scooted my chair out from the table. "How dare you sit up there and say that isn't you, you know da*! well that's you. You made it seem like everything with us was cool, you made me feel like my schedule did not bother you. I knew as soon as you joined that motorcycle club you were gonna do some fowl s*#!. I knew it... I told you!"

I cried in disbelief.

Bert had been a heavy drinker when I first met him. When I realized it was beginning to be a problem, I gave him an ultimatum and he quit and had not drunk for over twelve years. However, once he joined this motorcycle club, he had been coming home smelling like alcohol. He told me he finally realized that he could drink sociably and keep it under control. I was so disappointed, but he assured me it would not be an issue. He promised. Yet here we were.

> **Suddenly Single Moment**
> **If a person does not deal with their life demons, they will resurface at some point.**
> *—Adrianne*

***

Bert and I met right after a major break up I had had from a horrific domestic violence relationship. He made it so comfortable to share, and he listened and made me feel like I was so important.

He was Caucasian, so I really did not see us being more than friends, but gradually he grew on me.

He was nice to me, and I knew that if he ever tried to get physical, I could beat his ass. I know this sounds crazy, but I felt like it was a safe relationship, at least from physical abuse.

Bert had grown up around a lot of black guys, so he had a black swag about him. His conversation, his demeanor, his dress was all very urban.

Some would get offended by it but he was comfortable with who he was and was very loyal to his friends no matter what color they were or where they were from.

When we met, I knew that it was way too soon for me to jump into a relationship. Against my therapist's wishes, I moved forward with dating Bert.

Instantly I began changing or adjusting somethings about him. I wasn't really thrilled about his dress code, so I started changing his wardrobe. I hooked him up with a job through some friends and then encouraged him to start his own business. I obtained fleet accounts for him and promoted his business on social media.

Over the years I did all I could to put him a position to lead our home so he would be a good example to my children who both my son and daughter adored.

He grew on my family too, they absolutely loved him. So often when I thought the relationship was boring and my needs were not being met, I remained loyal and stuck by his side.

Through multiple health concerns, one which was cancer: I stayed by his side. The relationship was not intimate at all. No romance, no sex and if we did it was very minimal and compared to other relationships just unsatisfying.

But I loved him and stuck by his side through it all. Which is why it hurt so bad for me to see pictures of him with another woman. Like dude really? You ain't that cute, your sex is wack and what you have and who you are is only because of me. Not to brag or boast, and I did it all out of love for him... but I made you fool.

If we were together, I wanted him to be the best version of himself. Even his Mama, who I loved dearly, was so happy that I was a woman who seemed to motivate and inspire him to be a better person, and this is how you repay me? A*#hole!!!

Anyway...

After I cussed him out for denying it was him in the picture. I could no longer look at his disgusting, lying face. He was sitting there red and would barely look up from the table. He made me want to throw up even though I was no longer violent and hardly ever resulted to fighting anymore. But I wanted to fight him and slap the sh*!# out of him.

I gathered my things and went upstairs to my room. Normally we would watch the news, or have discussion about our day, but I was done. I mean really done! He was nothing to me at this point. I felt like whatever feelings I had were left on that kitchen table.

That night I asked him to sleep in the extra room and to move in there till he could move out of the house. I laid up all night looking at the picture repeatedly. I cried in disbelief. I was hurt.

Why was I not enough? Clearly, she did not look better than me. The picture my class shared with me didn't show her whole face, but she had on a baseball hat holding down her wig. Let me stop, I really don't mean to talk about the lady and you'll later understand why.

* * *

A few days went by, and we barely talked. I continued going to work, conducting my classes, super embarrassed. I had not shared what had happened with anyone. I don't think anyone would have even believed it because everyone thought we were the best couple ever. Things were what they always seemed, but we respected each other, so I thought.

On about the fifth night of him sleeping in the other room, he came in my room and got in the bed. I didn't say anything. I scooted as far over to the edge as I could and curled up in a tight fetal position attempting to go to sleep. Even though I was done in my head, I missed what we had, and I missed him.

Jan Mitchell

We were almost back into our regular routine after about a week or two. We had decided we would try to work some of it out. At least the friendship.

It was August 27, 2019, when my class made me aware of the infidelity. For the next 4 months we were able to be cordial and occasionally laugh. He assured me he was not seeing the lady and it seemed like we were working towards fixing the problem.

At this point, we were eighteen years into our relationship so neither one of us wanted to just throw it away, or so I thought.

On December 15, 2019, Bert and his motorcycle club were giving out toys at the club house. Although I hated him being involved with the club, I loved the fact that they executed a lot of charitable events and helped the community.

I happened to be home writing curriculum for my classes and my dog got sick. My dog was a little Chihuahua, was older and had seizures from time to time. I was usually able to help him through it but this time he was not getting better, and it was scaring me.

I called Bert, back-to-back to back attempting to get him to answer to help me figure out what to do for our dog. I continued calling, and he refused to answer. It was starting to scare me but at the same time my intuition was telling me something was not right. All sorts of things were going through my head.

He finally answered, yelling, and going off on me about blowing his phone up. I could clearly tell he was showing out in front of someone, and I ain't the one you wanna embarrass or show out with!

Keep in mind I am an anger management teacher. The angel on my shoulder said, "Don't dare go up there, pick your battles."

But the devil on the other shoulder said, "Gurrrl he's getting smart and yelling, you better go up there and check that a*#."

Listening to the devil, and not the angel, off I went to check him. By now I am furious, and I am not using any of the skills I share with my girls. I was out of control and out of order.

I rolled that Yukon up there and busted a U-turn on two wheels, tires screeching. Bert heard my car, and when I pulled in the parking lot, he emerges from a car I did not recognize. In the car with him was the very same girl in the picture from August; I recognized the hat.

"Why the hell did you come up here?" he screamed.

At this point everything went black. I cussed, I fussed,

and I called him names. I asked the lady to roll her window down, but she refused. She continued looking forward and didn't want any parts of what was going on.

I told her; "I have no beef with you I just want to ask you a question."

Now there is a very crucial part that occurred, but I cannot mention. Just know I could have gone to jail.

By now, the guys inside the club had come outside to see what was going on. I did not care, I continued yelling obscenities and exposing some of his secrets. I was out of control to the point it scared **me**.

Someone, one of the club members, yelled my name, begging me to stop. The lady just sat there looking crazy. I went back to my truck, and I really wanted to sob. I wanted to break down and cry but I had to be strong.

I sat there for a minute, and I just observed. The lady finally got out of the car and began yelling at Bert. I couldn't make out what she was saying but she looked upset. I was glad she was upset.

Finally, she looked over and we made eye contact. I motioned her to come my way. Reluctantly she came over to my truck and I rolled the window down.

"I am sorry you had to be involved in this, I don't have a problem with you," I explained. I had questions I wanted answers to, so I asked. Before I knew it, she began disclosing everything.

She had met him at one of his appointments. He was called out to clean her mother's car. They talked and flirted with one another.

She said she travels a lot on her job, and she invited him to go along on a trip to Hawaii on October 30th. This happened to be our (Me and Bert's) anniversary.

They also traveled to Atlanta together. Keep in mind he and I never took one vacation in 17 years other than Vegas for car shows. I could not believe it.

I played it off, but there was a part of me that was devastated. My feelings were so hurt, and I was using all the strength in my body to hold back the tears. If nothing else, I thought this man would have protected my feelings and at least took her out of the area to cheat instead of humiliating me in a place where everyone knew me.

I was sooooo embarrassed. She shared so much including some health issues she was dealing with. She emphasized that it was just an emotional relationship and they had never been intimate.

"Yea right"

JAN MITCHELL

I thanked her for taking the time to speak with me and apologized for acting like a crazy woman. I thought my actions toward her were cool. Boy was I wrong.

Mr. Bert was not allowed to return home. With the firearms and other weapons I had in the house, I'm sure he knew better than to ask to come there and especially without a police escort.

All night his mom and I called one another. He called her and told her how I went off. I was really close to his mom, but she didn't take his side. She knew what he did was not cool and when she talked to him, she emphasized he should not come to the house.

The next day with very minimal sleep, I drug myself to work but had to leave early. All my coworkers could tell something very bad had happened. I was the person who dressed up for work and was "suited and booted" every day.

I looked like I had been hit by a truck. Eyes nearly swollen shut, no makeup and had barely combed my hair. This was not like me. I had never experienced emotional pain this deep.

His Mom called to check on me, but I had not shared anything with my family at this point. Once I arrived home, I climbed in the bed with my phone and a bottle of water. I looked for this lady he had cheated on me with and I found her on social media. I knew I should not have done it, but I sent her a friend request.

Right after I did it, I thought "That was probably **not** a good idea." She must have instantly called Bert because he called me.

"Adrianne, why would you send her a friend request?" He asked in the softest voice I ever heard. He was attempting to come at me gently. "She is very upset and told me I better tell that b*%#! to leave her alone," he explained.

"She said b*%#!???" I asked.

The timid scary looking heffa, with the lifted lace front wig on who was trying to be nice to me? I was nice to this chick and now she wanna jump bad?

Wow. I hated talking about other women. I really didn't wanna make fun of her, but my emotions were on ten and she called me a b*%#!?

Mind you, I probably shouldn't have friend requested her but as a woman to another hurting woman I thought we had built a little rapport. I guess not, my bad.

I told Bert to tell this heffa a few choice words and that she doesn't want no problems. I was trying to be nice to her. The fact that he rushed to her defense was crazy to me. 17 years in a relationship and here he is taking up for a woman he barely knows. This was not the Bert I knew. I told him he needed to plan to get his stuff out of the house and I hung up.

I laid there thinking about how financially challenging it was going to be for me to go from two incomes to just my little bit of money. I was not willing to reconcile, I was done and needed to figure it out.

We had come to an agreement that he would continue to pay his half of the mortgage (his rent) and I would continue storing his work equipment at the house until he could locate a place to live. This would give me some time to figure out what I would be doing. Moving? Selling? I did not know.

Some may feel it was quick to try and figure it all out, but I needed a plan. Mentally I was struggling, emotionally I was broken, and spiritually I was angry. Why would God allow this to happen to me, as good as I have been to people?

WHY????

***

I pulled the covers over my head and fell asleep, then I slept some more. I only got out of the bed to go to the bathroom. I didn't bathe, I didn't answer or return calls. I was severely depressed, and I had never been

SUDDENLY *Single*

like this. Not even from the abusive relationship I had endured. I felt like I was going to die.

> **Suddenly Single Moment**
> -God does not withhold tests and trials from our lives. He does it to try and test our faith. Oftentimes when we get comfortable, God must test our trust in Him.
>
> *-Adrianne*

Bert called, his mother called, and the tough part was when my mom called. She had been talking to Bert's mom who told her that I was probably going to need some help. She knew I was a mess and very depressed.

After four days, I had finally mustered up enough courage to tell my mom everything that happened. She was so disappointed in Bert. She loved him and my whole family was in disbelief. "If he didn't want to be with you, he should have said so. He had no regards for your feelings."

My mom loved Bert so this hurt her bad too. You could tell she was angry but very sad for me.

JAN MITCHELL

The Healing Process

By now, my hair is matted to the back of my head from lying in bed for days. I've barely bathed, same clothes on for five days and I had not eaten anything. Just drank water.

All of this was way out of character for me. It was suggested I see a therapist or a counselor. On top of everything else I was missing my girls at the center. My students from my parenting, domestic violence and anger management classes all reached out to me. But the CEO of the agency said I could not come back for at least ninety days because I was sick.

I thought I could use this experience to teach the girls because I felt like they could learn from it. But she said no.

This was a lot to take on all at once. The person I loved and the thing I loved to do the most was all gone at the same time, and no one seemed to think it was that bad. My heart was crushed, and I was a mess.

There was nothing to fight over in our separation. Bert and I had been together for over seventeen years but the house was in my name. We made purchases together, but nothing was joint.

We were considered domestic partners, but this was only for medical insurance purposes. Bert had some medical concerns and one that I mentioned earlier was a bout he had with cancer. I stuck right by his side through the entire ordeal. None of this required us to go before a judge to figure out, we tried to keep things amicable and fair even now.

I struggled for months with depression. There was a period my insecurities and low self-esteem were out of control. I constantly measured myself against this woman who was nothing like me physically. She seemed to be an educated woman and smart, but her physical appearance was very basic. Not unattractive, just way different from me.

I don't know why I thought she is or ever was better than me. I needed help dealing with these issues. I had come a long way with building my self-esteem and getting over my insecurities but now I found myself back at square one. I decided to get some professional help because I needed it at this point.

It was always hard to start therapy for me, but I needed to get help immediately. I was under one hundred and forty pounds and for a woman of my stature this was not a good look. I looked sick, my hair was falling out, my nerves were bad, and I had no energy. I literally felt like I was dying.

I began doing something so weird. I began posting pictures excessively on social media looking for validation. I needed someone to tell me I was pretty; and a good person and they were proud of me. I met people but didn't really date. I was new to this single life, and it was quite scary.

I met an individual who just had experienced a breakup too and he was so cool. Ironically, he was in a Motorcycle Club too. I called him RB. He was funny, smart, and brutally honest. We spent nearly every day together just as friends initially. I cried, he cried. He really wanted to reconcile his relationship with his girlfriend, so respectfully kept my distance and maintained just being cool buddies. RB gave the best advice and even though I had gotten skinny and sickly he constantly told me I was beautiful, and I needed that.

I enrolled in a group class as well as one-on-one sessions for therapy Because I had a counseling background, in the beginning, I shut down and wasn't participating like I should have. I thought to myself, I already know this stuff. As a matter of fact, the teacher used some of the same handouts I used for my classes.

It was not until I embraced the seriousness of trying to heal that I began feeling better. I started participating and became honest and shared in groups openly and honestly with my therapist. I learned I was still dealing with past traumas.

I learned how it could have been my lack of attention to Bert which caused him to stray. Well, she did not say that, but she constantly asked what we did together. I felt like we had good communication and although I worked fourteen-hour days, I always asked him if I was doing too much? He consistently said no and how proud of me he was excited about my events and book signing and he supported everything I did.

I made sure we had date nights and suggested going on trips, but he always said he hated flying. Yet he and "the lady" had been to Hawaii on our anniversary, yes you heard me right **OUR** anniversary. They had been to Atlanta, up north, Oakland, San Francisco and more.

In 5 months, they had done more together than we had ever done. I was a little hurt by that. Why was I not enough? What was wrong with me that he didn't take **me** on vacations?

* * *

I was healing and getting better one day at a time. I had friends and family rooting for me. RB was my main support system. Therapy was helping both of us, we held each other accountable and before you know it the sadness was subsiding. I was ready to move on.

JAN MITCHELL

Against my therapist suggestion and after holding out as long as I could, RB and I had an intimate moment. I tried so hard just to be his friend, neither one of us was ready for a relationship, we were still healing. But no regrets, not even today. We are still very tight.

Therapy taught me so much about myself, I had not healed from previous trauma. I did not have healthy boundaries and I still was broken, with insecurities. I had a lot of work to do.

The area I reside in and where Bert and I resided for seventeen years, we were both very well known. So, when word got out that we were no longer together it was a shock to many.

Things can often look one way on the outside and be a mess inside. I really didn't feel we had a mess, I thought it was a health issue and I was sticking by my man. I was so wrong and stayed far too long. As I had in previous relationships, I remained longer than I should've. I loved his family, he loved mine, but we apparently stayed for all the wrong reasons

In my healing, I needed to own my part. I buried myself in my work, doing the stuff I loved to do because quite frankly the relationship began to get boring. I am certain my anger and depression did not really stem from the infidelity but more so from the embarrassment and the betrayal.

SUDDENLY *Single*

* * *

I am taking it one day at a time because I'd be lying if I said I still don't have days I want revenge. Instead, when Bert calls and needs a favor, I assist. If someone calls and needs his number for business, I provide it.

I have not talked to his mother, and I am hurt by that because I loved her so much. I have not forgiven her completely because she knew he was in this relationship and did not disclose it to me. She never gave me a "heads up."

His mom and I used to text or talked weekly sometimes a few days a week and to know she condoned his behavior really hurt my feelings. She knew of "the lady" they had met. Honestly, I have nothing against that woman, I tried to remain cordial, I came at her very kindly. It's an uncomfortable situation today but I deal with it. This to is part of my healing.

In a situation like this, those who become toxic you must find the strength to let go and let God. Seeking revenge does not help your healing process and those of us who are true believers know, 'no evil deed goes unpunished.'

"Vengeance is mine," says the Lord, "I will repay." I also remind myself that 'you reap what you sow.'

Jan Mitchell

I was the ANGER MANAGEMENT facilitator for 10 years and now I must utilize the same information I shared with my students. I've had to pull out my folders and use the same techniques I share with the women I served.

"Pick your battles."

> **Suddenly Single Moment**
> -No matter how you were wronged, allow the Lord to fight your battles. But choose your battles wisely.
>
> —*Adrianne*

With this along with therapy, I am on my way to full recovery. Working on ourselves must be constant until the casket closes. We should always be striving to be a better person than we were yesterday.

Sometimes you are caught off guard and shocked when love falls apart. Remember, don't rush the healing process. If possible, it's best to hold off on new relationships and intimacy until you change your mindset and set healthy boundaries.

I have not given up on "happily ever after." But I must deal with the pain of '**SUDDENLLY** Single' first.

SUDDENLY *Single*

Thank you for allowing me to share my story. My goal has always been to TURN MY MESS into a MESSAGE.

Break ups are hard, and you almost always experience the five stages of grief just like losing a loved one: denial, anger, bargaining, depression, and acceptance.

My prayer is that you seek help when needed, be patient with the process and take care of yourself.

God Bless!

XXOOXX

Adrianne

"Healing is a choice. The thing you fear most has no power. Your fear of it is what has the power. Facing the truth really will set you free."

~Oprah Winfrey

SUDDENLY *Single*

WHAT WAS I LOOKING FOR?

Knock, Knock.

My ex-husband: Who is it?

It's the Henry County Sheriff department.

He was afraid to open the door, so he put me, his WIFE to this fleeting task. That is a whole issue all within itself, but we will stick with the storyline for now. It probably made sense for me to answer the door since they were looking for **me**.

I opened the door and learned that the police were indeed looking for me as the offending party. About two to three months prior to this knock on my door, I had written a bad check for our marriage license, and the sheriff department was there to justify my actions. They verified it was me, announced why they were knocking on my door, and then put me in handcuffs. I was being arrested for fraud.

JAN MITCHELL

I was walked outside for the whole neighborhood to gaze upon. This preacher, woman of God was escorted in the back of a police car to pay the dues of her actions.

Why did it feel like this day EVERYONE was outside watching me? How was the most innocent person in my apartment complex being arrested?

Embarrassed.
Humiliated.
Shocked.
Angry.
Confused.

Was this the price of love? Had love cost me an overnight stay in a jail cell? We were not ninety days into the marriage, and I was learning the hard way I had made the worst decision of my life and God was **NOT** in it.

> **Suddenly Single Moment**
> -When God sends you signs early in the relationship, do not ignore them! Do more watching than praying!
> *-Audrea*

Love had blinded me very early on. He told me he loved me, and foolishly, I believed him because he was a very good friend from a previous season of my life. But that friendship was never meant to be exchanged for a marriage license. Especially one that threw me in jail.

I ended up spending the night in jail because I was arrested on a Sunday and the court would resume the next day. It made no sense to spend money for bail when that money would pay off the fines and court costs I had racked up from my night in jail.

The next day, the judge allowed me to plead No-lo, which meant not pleading guilty or innocent. He ordered me to pay the fees and costs and go home. It seemed like he could not understand why I was arrested in the first place for such a petty crime. I was told it would not end up on my record, but it showed up at an inopportune time and I lost a job behind it.

That is another story for another day.

***

What happened? I was supposed to spend the rest of my life and into eternity with this man. But somehow things didn't turn out the way I thought. I **thought** he loved me. I **thought** he really had my best interest at heart. But what I learned was it was all a web of deception, and it was unweaving before my very eyes.

Before I tell you how I became **SUDDENLY** single,

allow me to share the lies that brought me to this point....

It was the end of the year 2011 and I had had enough, mind you we wed in 2010. He promised he would do better, things would get better, and he even promised he would do his part to help pay the bills. But what he was doing was digging me into a deeper hole that became harder to come out of.

The year was ending, and I gave him an ultimatum. I wrote him a letter and I told him he had exactly twelve months to get himself together and seek therapy to gain the healing he needed to elevate his life. If not, I was divorcing him for good. I don't think that he took my threats seriously, but it was what I had to do because I couldn't take it anymore.

What I learned prior to this threat is he was bi-polar, had been off his meds and his testosterone levels were way below normal. This was what he claimed caused him to go in and out mentally, become depressed and move into our spare bedroom. His actions left me feeling alienated, not understanding what was going on or what I had done.

He swore it was not me, it was him. But *why* had he not sought the counseling and therapy he needed to mend his life?

SUDDENLY *Single*

> **Suddenly Single Moment**
> **-A person not willing to work on themself is a person not ready to work on a marriage.**
>
> *—Andrea*

***

Allow me to backtrack for a moment...

He came for a visit and that visit turned into a marriage ceremony. It was not supposed to be this way. We were planning a beautiful fall wedding and marrying before our planned date was not on my agenda.

If I could be totally honest, we had had premarital sex and I wanted to make my sex legal. I figured well, we're going to get married so we may as well go ahead and do it now. This way, we don't have to repent for our actions.

But what I learned is that it was all a part of the web he was weaving to get me into his lair. You see, when he came to my place, he never had intentions to leave. He knew if he sexed me up well enough, it would cause me to make irrational decisions.

He understood the psychological and physical state I was in. I had been celibate for ten+ years at that point and one lick of the cookie would cause me to fall into his trap. According to his calculations, he would be in a secure place.

She has a beautiful home. She keeps it clean. She has a great job, making good money. Her bills are paid. She drives a practically brand-new car. Yes, I can settle my feet here.

It was a precisely calculated plan.

He played a very good role at first, I must give him credit. He paraded around like he loved the Lord and wanted to answer the call of God on his life. But that role soon became a bad act when I discovered he was still living a homosexual lifestyle in the background.

In more recent conversations with him he swears he was not living that lifestyle and he really desired to change. If a person desires to change, they will do the work necessary for change to occur. He was not willing to do the work, but I was.

Although our marriage got off to a very bad start, I was willing to do what it took to make it work. When I said, "I do," it was for life. I never imagined getting married and even considering divorce. Divorce was never in the cards in my mind. But when you have someone not willing to get in the fight *with* you, you most likely will end up fighting alone.

SUDDENLY *Single*

There were numerous occurrences which brought me to my **SUDDENLY** single state...

It was checking my computer and learning he visited homosexual websites. This led to a conversation where he **said** he wanted to change but continued his actions. He even entertained conversations on social media where he attempted to date a local man in our area.

When the man confronted him about the photos circulating of my ex and I's wedding, he told lies to convince him we were not that serious: I was not fulfilling his needs.

Yes, I snooped into his DM.

It was also the constant emotional and financial abuse he inflicted on my banking account, disrupting my whole life and routine. It was not paying the bills on time. It was him not producing stable income to help with the household bills. It was him encouraging me to write checks when the money was not in our account.

He would say, "Oh you get paid Friday, it won't clear before then." These were his poor spending habits, not mines.

These same habits landed **me** in jail.

Jan Mitchell

It was all a mess. The odd thing or should I say the crazy thing is that his mind never computed the fact that he was destroying my life minute by minute hour by hour and day by day.

> **Suddenly Single Moment**
> -A person who does not own anything has no value for what you have worked so hard to build.
> —*Andrea*

* * *

Back to when I said I was gonna leave right? You remember, the twelve-month warning I gave him?

I can now look back and say that I made a poor choice by up and leaving my home. The mistake I made was when I gave him the warning, I went and stayed at my sister's house. I left him in the house furnished with items from **my** labor and that of my deceased mother. I should not have left my home, but I couldn't see any other way to get out of the situation I was in.

Here I was separated from the man who I was supposed to spend the rest of my life with, but we were no longer on track for our, 'forever.'

I found myself sleeping on my sister's couch because I needed to alleviate myself of the toxic environment created in my home. Not only was I sleeping on her couch, but I was experiencing the horrible transition of living alone **again**.

As a result of the breakup, I broke out in hives all over my body with black marks all over my face, torso, legs and everywhere. This was a direct indication that I was now **SUDDENLY** broken from this marriage, the covenant I had made.

I think the worst part of the separation was dealing with the hives that broke out all over my body: it was painful. It hurt to take a shower. It hurt to take a bath and it just hurt because my soul was shattered in pieces from this horrible arrangement my life had become.

I can honestly say that my life pieces did not start coming together until the divorce was final even after leaving and being separated for twelve+ months.

His mouth said he was wanted our marriage to work although he was doing **nothing** to put in the work for us to reunite. I had to face the painful reality that he was not willing to love me as he had vowed on our wedding day. I was ready for counseling, therapy or whatever it took, but his effort went lacking.

He says I didn't wait for him; I didn't pray for him, and I did not fight hard enough for him. As I look back, he didn't fight hard enough for **himself**.

Jan Mitchell

Healing Is My Portion

After almost eight years divorced, and writing for this book, my healing hit me in the face.

When I separated from my ex, I became a nomad. Moving from place to place just because I could, and I had no obligations that kept me locked to one location. It felt great to be free! When I traveled, I could clear my head and think about my hopes, dreams, and my future.

Not my reality. I got lost in the travel.

It was 2021 when I realized that I was *tired* of all the moving around. I had finally come to terms with *why* I was moving around. I was looking for the love I lost when I became **SUDDENLY** single.

I had made the commitment to my ex, and that covenant was broken. Subconsciously, I was roaming around looking for the love I had lost.

Yeah, I know: Reality check.

It was during was a conversation with my close guy friend when I expressed why I had been moving around so much. Subconsciously, I was in a desperate need to find someone who would **love**, **appreciate**, and **accept** me.

Although my ex had his flaws, he had a love for me that melted my heart away. It was not until these moments when I realized this type of love was missing from my world.

This *is* the sort of love you receive from a husband, but it cannot be tainted, or the lines of respect will be lost.

Just like that, God healed me, and gave me permission to close this chapter of my life. Never to reopen, but to move forward, realizing that this type of love exists for me without pretense, ill motives, or manipulation.

When you allow healing to occur, and trust the Father, He will release this love to you in **His** timing.

It's called pragma love.

Wait on it.

XXOOXX

Andrea

"Closure happens right after you accept that letting go and moving on is more important than projecting a fantasy of how the relationship could have been."

~Sylvester McNutt

IN SICKNESS AND IN HEALTH

*"Jan, I did not promise you that **man** would not leave you. But I, Myself, have said that I will never leave you nor forsake you. But I need you to trust Me."*

Face deeply tear-stained from hours of weeping and great weariness of soul, I tiredly replied, "Lord, I trust You for a lot of things, but this one right here...I don't know."

* * *

September 18, 2015, was the day the trajectory of my life would change forever. A year prior, Steve, the girls, and I stopped by my mom's house. My oldest sister, my brother-in-law and my nephew stopped by as well and we all sat around talking, eating, and laughing.

Steve was a jolly and boisterous man from Arkansas, standing at six feet, two inches and two hundred and twenty-four pounds who loved to laugh and joke constantly. He was one of those people who never met a stranger and you always felt safe with him.

As we were talking, a deep, concerned look came over my mother's face. My sister and I noticed it immediately. Mom began crying and trembling. My Mom isn't a crier, so to see her weep uncontrollably caused a bit of anxiety for me and my sister.

"Mom, what's wrong?! What is it?! Are you hurting?" Christy asked.

Mom just shook her head "no" and kept rocking. Steve, being who he was, jumped up to hug Mom and said, "Aww, Mom, everything is going to be alright."

I looked at Steve and shook my head because I understood that this wasn't something that could be explained naturally: Mom was having a spiritual experience. My mother had a strong sense of discernment through the gift of the Holy Spirit, and I could sense it was one of those moments.

My brother-in-law looked at Steve and said, "Hey man, let's take the kids outside for a walk."

As the men gathered the children and everyone went outside, Mom looked at me. My sister held Mom and asked, "Mom, is this the same feeling you had before our cousin 'Bryan' got killed in the car accident last year?"

Mom nodded, 'yes.'

As the door closed shut, she began trembling again and said, "It's Steve. Something is going to happen to him." And with that, she started crying again.

> **Suddenly Single Moment**
> -Whenever a life altering situation will occur, God will provide a warning. Make sure to heed the warning no matter how painful.
> -Jan

* * *

Steve had a history of lupus and with it came grand mal seizures amongst many other ailments. From Raynaud's disease to neuropathy in his legs and feet. Steve's lupus and seizures were well managed with therapeutic and medicinal measures.

Yet, as I sat there listening to Mom, I felt dread hit the pit of my stomach. I knew that when Mom had these Holy Spirit-inspired insights, it would come to pass. As was normal for me, I didn't give way to my feeling, but rather, put on my stoic face and said, "Mom, I'm taking care of Steve and he's doing his part to make sure that he's staying healthy."

My reassuring words fell on deaf ears to both my mom as well as myself. My words felt empty to my ears as again, I knew that when Holy Spirit speaks, it is a sure deal.

* * *

It's now August 18, 2016, and Steve and I are attending a church conference event that hosted many guest singers. It was an opportunity to get out and listen to good gospel music and fellowship with others in the church community. We were able to get away for the evening: just the two of us.

Steve and I were a blended family of four daughters; I came with two (Korii and Zian), Steve came with one (Lisa) and we had one together (Ava). Ava was just seven months old at the time and a handful, so the night away was much welcomed.

As we dropped the girls off to hang out with my mom for the evening, Mom took a real good look at me and Steve.

"You all look so nice. You're glowing. There seems to be a radiant glow about you two."

We thanked Mom, hugged the girls, and headed out. The night was nice, the conference was okay, and we were ready to leave before the service ended. I noticed Steve was happy but seemed a little less talkative and engaging as he normally was.

On those days, I would brace myself for how the evening might turn out. Most times when he was quieter than usual, it would be a precursor to a night of bedtime seizures.

Over the past few months, despite being faithful to his daily medication regimen, Steve would still have breakthrough seizures, sometimes up to four to five a night within an hour apart each time.

Steve had many specialists from the state's best rheumatologist to a hematologist (for thrombocytopenia- another lupus side effect), a neurologist and so many more. Thankfully, that night, I was able to get a full night's rest and even a little intimacy from Steve that evening.

* * *

Sunday, September 18, 2016, our little family traveled to church, which was our norm as Steve was one of the church ministers and Sunday school teachers. Our beautiful little church was few in numbers, but powerful in teaching and the Spirit.

I would occasionally play the drums (I only had one beat that I could fully hang with). Steve led the morning prayer which would begin our normal services following Sunday school. It was a powerful prayer where you could feel the anointing resonating off Steve.

When he finished praying, the Pastor walked calmly to the podium and stated, "Satan is going to attack someone in here, but he will not prevail!"

With that declaration, the entire congregation went up in a praise of warfare. As we began to praise, I began singing the old congregational song, "Whatever you need, God's got it!"

As I began singing, the anointing overtook the place and a lady from the back began to dance her way down the aisle. Seeing her praise made me think, "Oh, she must be the one who the word of warning is for!"

I began to praise with her by playing my tambourine and dancing with her. Little did I know later that same evening, I would learn my praise and the warning were confirming what my mother had prophesied a year earlier, and what our Pastor and guest Evangelist revealed.

The praise and the Word were for me and the strength I would need. As usual, Steve sat and ate dinner with us before he would head out to pick up the Pastor and a few other ministers to go to prison ministry.

SUDDENLY *Single*

Steve kissed me as he left, and I knew that it would be around 9:30 PM or 10:00 PM that night before he would return. The drive to the prison was nearly an hour and a half away.

Ten o'clock came and I could hear Steve entering the hallway of our apartment where we lived at the time. Suddenly, I heard a sickening, guttural scream escape Steve's mouth: I knew that yell.

It was the sound he would make before having a grand mal seizure. The girls and I quickly ran to unlatch the door and run into the hallway to assist. As I swung the door open, Steve was already in mid-fall. I ran to catch him, but logic raised up and reminded me, "He's six two and two hundred twenty-four pounds. Right now, his body is dead weight, so if you try to catch him, both of you will be seriously hurt!"

I listened to reason and stopped in place. I could also see that there was enough open space in the hall that if he fell, he would hurt his shoulder, as he was falling sideways. He had had both a hip replacement and shoulder replacement within the first year of our marriage: compliments of lupus.

As I watched, in what seemed like "slow-motion," Steve's body took another jerk, directing his head to the wall. He slammed his head into the wall so hard, it made a dent in the drywall.

JAN MITCHELL

I don't even remember opening my mouth to scream, but I heard myself scream. It was like an outer body, surreal experience. My scream was so loud that my neighbor ran to her door to see what was wrong. She didn't open the door, just asked, "Is everything okay?!"

I could hardly talk as I thought Steve had cracked his skull. "We need... I need...get an ambulance!'

My neighbor opened her door and advised, "Don't move him!"

I am so glad I listened as I later learned that moving him would have cost his life at that moment. As the ambulance arrived, which seemed to take forever, I rushed into the house to call my mom and asked her to come and stay with the girls while I followed the ambulance.

I got dressed and ran out the door, hearing my then nine-year-old, Zian, quietly sobbing in her room, looking out the window as they carried her "Dad" away.

Driving speedily behind the ambulance, I arrived and quickly parked in the "Emergency" parking lot of St. Vincent's Trauma 1 Unit. I didn't know what to expect as I quickly checked in with the front desk and was ushered to Steve's room.

As I headed in, the clinical staff rushed me out advising that they needed to get Steve back to radiology for cat scans and an x-ray. An hour later, they returned with Steve and allowed me to come back into the room.

The attending physician began wiggling Steve's toes and touched his arms. "Can you feel me touching you?" the physician asked.

Steve, tearfully, shook his head, "no."

"I didn't think so. You broke your neck badly. It's broken in three places," stated the physician.

Again, I heard myself gasp as I don't recall opening my mouth. My body felt limp, and it seemed as if the room was spinning. I had never fainted in my life, but at that moment, I felt like I was going to. The attending physician asked the nurse to take me out of the room and give me something to drink.

As the nurse walked me down the hall to the dreaded "family room," she asked if I needed to call anyone. I quickly whipped out my phone and began stumbling through dialing my mom's digits first.

"Mom, I need you…I need everybody. Get up here! Steve broke his neck!"

The next call was to my pastor and his wife, who also were stunned with disbelief as I mumbled gibberish about what was happening. The last call was to Lisa and then to Steve's mom and family in Arkansas.

I couldn't breathe. I couldn't feel. I couldn't comprehend all the emotions that were overwhelming me at that moment.

My life had changed in an instant. I had woken up that day a young, vibrant wife and mother and now instantly I was a caregiver. My husband had broken his C5-C7 with a facet jump. He was declared a complete quadriplegic.

From that day forward, I would not only be caring for my young girls but also my 46-year-old husband. Long gone would be the days of easily rolling over to him in bed for a night of passion, as he was now disabled and unable to perform, much less stand the pressure of me being in bed with him.

Lupus further exacerbated the issue, causing Steve a longer stay than we originally anticipated. Typically, if one survives such a tragic spinal cord injury, the neck can be fused, and the patient is sent to rehab within a week. Not so with lupus.

Steve's stay extended for thirty days in the Neuro Trauma ICU, where he flatlined on four different occasions. Due to the extent of his injuries, Steve needed a tracheostomy, a feeding tube, and a respirator.

The attending physician recommended Steve to a cardiothoracic surgeon for a pacemaker, but through prayer, it was discovered that one of the new seizure medications the hospitalist assigned to Steve was causing his heart to stop.

Before being revived after one of Steve's "deaths," where he was down for twenty-three minutes, he told me the following: "Jan, I died. I saw myself in the casket and you had planned the funeral. But then, I heard this great, BIG voice say, 'You're not going anywhere because you've got work to do!'"

With that, Steve and I both burst into tears for we knew the "big" voice he had heard was God's. We thought that meant God was going to heal Steve miraculously and we were going to share with the world how God had done such great things!

* * *

After five long months of hospitals, rehabs, nursing homes, and sometimes, negligent staff, I traveled back and forth daily to advocate and make sure that Steve was being treated right by the clinical staff. God blessed Steve to see his forty seventh birthday, watch Ava take her first steps, and celebrate her first birthday. We also celebrated all the major winter holidays, including New Year. We celebrated each celebratory moment at the medical establishment.

February 2017 rolled in and as Steve and I were discussing his next moves to yet another rehab with the nurse case manager, I heard Holy Spirit whisper, "I need you to return to college to get your degree in healthcare."

I was taken aback as I had dropped out of college during my freshman year over ten years ago, when I became pregnant with my firstborn.

I later returned to a local community college and obtained my Dental Assisting license, where I made the Dean's list. Then I determined that wasn't the career fit for me, so I settled with working a good job that paid me enough to be comfortable and take care of my family.

Now, I was hearing this in my conscience. I quietly responded, "Lord, I hope that you're not asking me to be a Nurse!"

Steve had developed stage four bedsores during his various stays that were so deep the nurse could put her hand inside up to her wrist. I learned how to clean his bed wounds, turn him, provide the quad-assist push to help him cough up any lodged mucous, clean his trach, insert a catheter and my stomach could not take it.

SUDDENLY *Single*

Yet, I was willing to do whatever it took to take care of my man. But there were many days, I was exhausted. I had seen enough. I was praying that nursing was not what God was asking me to do!

* * *

Within minutes, the physician walked in and advised that Steve would begin an antibiotic as he had developed an infection from the nursing home staff where he attended before being sent back to the hospital.

After a few days of Steve being on the antibiotic I noticed he seemed drowsier than he had previously been when he had taken antibiotics. He had developed MRSA and Cdiff previously, so antibiotics weren't new to him.

This round on the antibiotics, his body's response time was different. When I mentioned this to the doctor, she began speaking with me and Steve.

"Something rare has happened and I want to prepare you all for the worst that could happen. Somehow, Steve got stool in his bedsores while at the nursing home and the stool was found to be positive with Cdiff. The Cdiff traveled to his bloodstream, which is extremely rare. However, when it does get in the blood, it has a fifty percent mortality rate. I need to know what you all would like to do in case things turn for the worst. Do you want Steve to be placed back on the ventilator or would you like palliative care to provide a more comforting route?"

I couldn't digest what I was hearing. We thanked the doctor and asked for privacy to discuss among ourselves what to do. Steve laid back calmly in the hospital bed.

I leaned over and asked, "Babe, did you hear what the doctor just said? What would you like for me to do?" Steve calmly replied, "I'm not worried because remember God said that I'm not going anywhere because I've got work to do!"

As soon as Steve finished speaking, the Holy Spirit whispered to me, "Let him know that he's already done his work. Remind him of the encouragement he's given to others and my word that he's shared with all the clinical staff since he's been hospitalized and able to speak. Remind him of all the men that he's ministered to at the prison. Remind him!"

I did just that.

As I recounted to Steve all that Holy Spirit advised, Steve closed his eyes with a smile of contentment on his face.

That night I attended the nursing home where Steve and I and a few of the other members from our church would go to share the good news of the gospel and sing.

> **Suddenly Single Moment**
> -When the Holy Spirit advises you to give a word of encouragement, give the word in peace.
> You never know what is at stake for someone's soul.
>
> -Jan

I didn't want to go because my mind was still reeling from the news the doctor shared with us. I pressed my way and as I began to go forth in song and word, I felt a supernatural strength that graced me to deliver with precision and clarity. I have never praised and worshipped so hard. The team and I left refreshed and encouraged as well as the residents.

I made a quick stop back by the hospital to advise Steve of that night's service before heading home to be with the girls. Around eleven pm when I turned over in bed, there was a song playing in my head, "God is my everything," by the Chicago Mass Choir.

I couldn't shake the song out of my spirit, especially the lyrics, "He's my joy in sorrow. He's my hope for tomorrow."

I finally threw the covers back and said to myself, "Let me go find this song and play it so that I can get it out of my system and go back to bed!"

As I played the song, I began dancing in worship in my living room. As I was praising God, a sudden heaviness hit me, and I sat down.

"God, what is going to happen to Steve? Is he going to live or die? I need to know. You know that I don't like surprises."

It took a moment of silence from the Holy Spirit and a few more dance steps before I heard the Holy Spirit's answer, "I am going to heal Steve, but not the way you were expecting or praying for."

I responded, "God, I need you to talk plain to me. What are you telling me?"

The Holy Spirit spoke again, "I'm going to take him."

I screamed.

This time, I remembered opening my mouth. I screamed and cried so loud that I had to grab a sofa pillow to cover my mouth so my daughters would not hear me wailing.

I laid prostrate across the floor and began pleading with God to spare Steve's life. I didn't consider nor care that I was being selfish. I later realized that the matter was already settled between God and Steve. There had been a conversation between the two of them that I was not privy to.

I just wanted Steve.

How was I going to explain this to my daughters? How was I going to explain to my mother-in-law, who started believing earlier rumors from troublemaking in-laws and "out-laws?" She had listened to the lies of an envious in-law who told her that I attempted to murder Steve. They claimed after Steve caught me cheating that I pushed him down the stairs, that we didn't even have. We lived on the first floor. There was no other man, outside of Jesus.

Steve and I had only been married for five and a half years at that point. I wasn't expecting to be a widow this soon. I recalled when we recited our vows, "For better or for worse. In sickness and in health. Til death do us part."

I didn't expect death to show up at our door such a short time later. I had never planned a funeral before. How was I going to manage this? Why was I being thrust into being a single mother again? Was God repaying me for my earlier illicit trysts that I'd had **before** I got married? What was going on?

Jan Mitchell

I continued pleading and crying out to God until five am the next day. I had no more strength in my body to fight. I had exhausted all my prayer vocabularies. I had no more tears left to cry.

As I lay quiet in a pool of tears, I gave one last attempt to ask God for Steve's life. God gently reminded me that He loved Steve with an everlasting love that was greater than any love any human could give him combined. He reminded me that He said that He was going to heal Steve, which meant that Steve would make it in. He reassured me that He was going to take great care of Steve.

Finally, as I lay whimpering, the Holy Spirit spoke, "Jan, I never promised you that man would not leave you. But I, Myself, have said that I will never leave you nor forsake you. But, I need you to trust Me."

At that moment, I reluctantly surrendered my will and told God that I would trust Him in this matter, but I let Him know that I didn't like it.

The moment I surrendered, I received a phone call from the hospital that they were having a difficult time waking Steve up using the sternum rub method and that I needed to get to the hospital right away. I called my family and rushed to the hospital.

Steve awakened that day, but within four days he took his last breath. As I made the calls of the announcement of his passing to his family, his mother cursed me out and told me to take my 'da*#' hands off her son. I pulled the phone away from my ear as she continued to rage in her grief and anger.

Once she calmed down, I let her know that I would give her time to come to the hospital. She was already traveling to Indiana to visit Steve as she knew that he was in his final hours, yet she delayed a day.

I leaned over, grabbed Steve's lifeless body in an embrace, and kissed his lips which were still as warm and soft as our last kiss, I remembered. My mother and two friends from church were in the room with me at the time of his passing.

As Steve's family began to flood the hallways and room, my family and I began to leave out. At that point, I knew that it would be a volatile situation as emotions were at an all-time high for all of us. I walked out of the hospital; I was numb. I walked down the cold hallway to my car surrounded by both my biological and church family.

* * *

The next morning, I received a phone call of condolences from the funeral home whom I instructed to conduct Steve's services.

As the director began to speak with me, she asked, "Did you arrange for a funeral home in Arkansas to host Steve's services?"

"No, I did not," I replied, sitting up straight in the bed. I didn't think so. I knew something was off. The family was here earlier at the funeral home rushing me to sign papers to release Steve's body.

The funeral director continued, "'Something,' told me to slow down and recheck the paperwork. That's when I saw you were listed on the death certificate as the next of kin."

Unbelievable. My mother-in-law had attempted to "steal" my husband's body and take him down to Arkansas without any communication with me. I thanked the director for letting me know and catching the issue. I was livid!

I told my family what happened, and everyone experienced the same frustration over the foolishness I was experiencing. My Pastor caught wind of the matter as some of my in-laws called him threatening to do bodily harm to me if I didn't release Steve's body. This further enraged me because I am not scared of anyone, and I certainly don't accept threats lightly.

Yet, the Holy Spirit!

He began to speak and reminded me of a saying that I would hear my late founding Pastor say, "It doesn't take power to talk! It takes power to shut your mouth sometimes."

I responded, "But, God, do you see this mess?!" He responded, "Stand still and see the salvation of the Lord. For these enemies that you see today, you will not see anymore."

"Are you sure, God?" I pressed.

"In quietness and confidence shall be your strength. I need you to trust Me."

I sighed.

I couldn't win it seemed. I told God, "Okay, what do you want me to do?"

The Holy Spirit prompted me not to fight over a body, but instead to call the funeral home and release Steve, I did so. He also prompted me through my sister to call my mother-in-law and thank her for sharing her son with me and give her my condolences.

Once I did, I felt a supernatural peace from God overtake me. I knew that God was carrying me because the load lifted, and it was as if no offense had even taken place.

I released Steve's body for his family to have his funeral in Arkansas. I did not attend his funeral.

However, I did host a powerful praise and worship memorial service for him, which all his local friends could attend.

The church was standing room only for we had the doctors, nurses, our lawyer, teachers, a few of the prisoners who had been released, plus our family flood the room. My worship was my release.

> **Suddenly Single Moment**
> -Gaining peace after becoming SUDDENLY Single may mean letting go. It does not always feel good to let go, but it's worth your peace.
> —Jan

***

Three months after Steve's services, I changed my career to one in healthcare. I became a patient access professional, who scheduled patient appointments for various doctor's clinics at a major hospital facility in Indiana.

For many days, in the beginning, I would cry as I drove to work because I remembered the reason I was in healthcare. God birthed my purpose and life assignment through the tragedy and death of Steve.

"Let me make this clear. A single grain of wheat will

never be more than a single grain of wheat unless it drops into the ground and dies. Because then it sprouts and produces a great harvest of wheat-all because one grain died."
-**John 12:24** (The Passion Translation, TPT).

My Healing Came Through Serving

Through Steve's many nights of being in the hospitals, rehabs, and nursing homes, I've gained a new awareness of what is broken in the healthcare system and needed to be fixed. I also gained a new understanding and compassion for patients and families who are thrown into emergency health situations and struggle with navigating the system. Some families may need additional assistance to make it through.

I gained new compassion for the overworked nursing and clinical staff and how they desire to help, but sometimes the "red tape" of healthcare laws prevents them from providing the full care they want to give.

In the time that I began as a patient access professional, I began receiving recognition and was featured in a few of the healthcare newsletters for the compassionate and excellent care I strive to show patients and the clinical staff, even behind a telephone.

Today, I am a Supervisor in Patient Access, and I have written a few articles for the National Association of Healthcare Access Management Journal. I was recently elected to sit on the Board of Directors as the Midwest Regional Delegate, where I represent the six states in the Midwest (US).

Sometimes, God will use the very thing that wounded you and send you back to be its healer. I am grateful for the time God allowed me to experience marriage with Steve. No matter how great your loss may be, you don't have to die because your loved one did.

Live on!

"So, we are convinced that every detail of our lives is continually woven together for good, for we are his loves who have been called to fulfill his designed purpose."
-**Romans 8:28** (TPT)

XXOOXX

Jan

THE POWER OF FORGIVENESS

I must admit, there aren't too many relationships I can say almost destroyed me.

In 1995, I was married to my first husband. I thought it was going to be a good one—little did I know. I was in an interracial relationship and that has its own battles. However, never would I have known the trial of faith and how close to the breaking point I would get.

But God....

My relationship with my ex-husband, Jr. started off fun and we were just friends. After about six months, he asked me to marry him, but I told him 'no' numerous times.

Yet, we still ended up husband and wife. The trials of being in an interracial marriage were tough, not because of the relationship itself but because of the people around us.

> **Suddenly Single Moment**
> -A relationship can only stand with a good support system. Be careful who you are surrounded by.
> —Kalala

* * *

We were married and all was well. I became pregnant after five months of being married. I already had a son who was four and now I was going to welcome another child.

I must say this is when things went wrong. I noticed that he would stay out with a friend of his; his wife and I were friends. When I was nine months pregnant, he would stay out all night saying that he was sitting by the water with a group of friends and lost track of time...

All night.

However, the Lord was telling and showing me otherwise. Nevertheless, I stayed.

SUDDENLY *Single*

Jr was in the military and would go out on deployment—sometimes for two months, four months and six months at a time. I felt like his times of deployment would be the hardest. I even thought moving out of town with his racist mother was going to be the worst but that did not compare to what was to come.

* * *

In 1997, I became pregnant with my third child. I had this feeling something was wrong. Jr would be on the phone whispering but then would go outside to finish his conversation.

Once, my daughter, who was around eighteen months, tried to follow him down the stairs. He was so enticed by the conversation he was having on the phone that he ignored her. She almost fell eighteen flights of stairs and I was so angry. However, I stayed through his neglect.

While I was married to Jr., this was the era of the almighty 'beeper.' One day, I decided to write all the numbers down from his beeper. I placed the paper in my purse and didn't think anything else of it.

A few days later, the day before Labor Day, he gave me the news. "I don't want to be with you anymore."

Jan Mitchell

He said this so bluntly, like as a matter of fact. I was stunned. "What do you mean, you don't want to be married?"

The pain that hit me was mixed with confusion. Here I was nine months pregnant with no job. This was the day I went into labor but did not know it. I guess I am telling you all of this to make a point.

Allow me to continue. I was in labor for twenty-four hours but assumed it was the pain of my heart. The next day, I went to my doctor's appointment, which meant I had to walk and push my eighteen-month-old baby all the way there.

I was alone.

No one would go with me, and no one would be with me when I got there. When I arrived, I was in active labor. I called my ex-husband and told him. He came by. Yes, I said, he came by.

I was left in labor alone. If it had not been for two different friends, I would have given birth alone. The first was a nursing student but she had to leave and go to work, and the other was a friend who was pregnant also.

It was so hard and painful. But those times I sat in the hospital alone, I was praying and hoping that someone would think of me and come see about me.

SUDDENLY *Single*

How and why was I in this relationship? As I laid there and cried, my baby was soon to come.

I was in the hospital for two days. I had my tubes tied because I had made up my mind that I would never go through anything like this again.

When it was time to go home, by grandmother took me next door to her house. She allowed me to stay there with my baby.

Note: my other kids were with my aunt out of town. This was so that I could focus on healing.

* * *

Well, I had those numbers that I had written out of my ex-husband's beeper. I called a friend and asked her to dial and ask for him.

I started at the bottom of the list...nothing. We started calling at the top of the list...nothing.

It was that middle number on the list.

When we asked for Jr., she told me to hold on. I immediately hung up on the phone with everyone. I called back and asked for him myself. The lady who answered the phone told me to hold on and she went and got him. My world had fell apart at that moment.

I was able to talk to the lady on the other end briefly. I told her who I was and about my baby. I also told her to bring him to me.

I was so hurt.

I wanted to hurt him like he hurt me. I sat outside with a bat and a baby. The neighbors called my grandmother and told her what I was doing. She came home and told me to go into the house. She stayed with me until the lady came and brought him to me.

> **Suddenly Single Moment**
> -A good support system will keep you from doing irrational things that could land you in jail.

* * *

I am the type of person who must be broken from a situation to release it: I was that person. Now I am not.

I went through months of being around them, listening to them, and watching them. The love I had for him turned to hate. I didn't want him breathing the air I was breathing.

The emotional trauma I endured during this time in

my life was horrible. Not only was I going through post-partum, but I was going through heart break. When my heart would beat, a sharp pain would go to my head.

Not only did he cause a breakup with me but apparently, he spoke with my grandmother, and she sided with him and told me that it was my fault. I was crushed even the more.

I thought about killing me and my kids, but the Lord sent someone to minister to me. This relationship caused me to give up. I went from being a mom with my kids to allowing my family to convince me to allow my kids to be with them until I got it together.

The pain of this—was more than I thought I could bear; however, it was as set up from the enemy. I went from this bad marriage into a horrible relationship with someone who sold drugs, cheated and then I sold drugs, went to jail, and became addicted to weed.

Healing In My New Beginning

When I met my current husband, I was at rock bottom. I had nothing or no one.

Jan Mitchell

My first marriage was over twenty years ago. I have now been remarried for nineteen years to a man who I never thought I would find. I am finally happy and in a good place.

When I look back over this point of my life, the Lord blessed me to help others in their marriage. I had to find my identity and it was not in a person but in God. My children are all grown. My oldest has a good job and is a musical artist (top sixty-seven on the charts in Brazil). My oldest daughter is having her second child and my youngest daughter, lives out of town and has her own family; no kids just a fiancé and dogs.

As far as my ex-husband, I have forgiven him, and we are friends. When he has an issue in life, he calls, and I pray and talk to him. I am thankful for the journey and thankful that the Lord has brought me thus far.

I pray this helps someone. You may be going through a tough time right now but stay encouraged. Healing is a process, and you will not be destroyed. You will find the strength that is within you.

May the Lord bless you all!!

XXOOXX

PUTTING THE PIECES TOGETHER

I will never forget this day: my twenty first birthday in Iraq.

After working twenty-six hours straight on a prison compound, I was searching for three detainees who had escaped. When all the chaos was over and the detainees were found, I finally had time to wind down and spend time with high-ranking intelligence: NCO, who I was secretly seeing.

I was sitting on the steps outside of our living quarters watching the sunset and reflecting over my life while venting to him about all the stress this deployment had caused.

I will never forget the words he spoke to me, "You are going to be someone special one day just watch. You are going to change this world."

Jan Mitchell

I couldn't get this day out my head. Sixteen years later and I still think about this day, and it feels like it was yesterday.

When I look back and put all the puzzle pieces together, it all makes sense. I have endured trials, tribulations, and high milestones but they were not meant for me to hide; but treasures and gems to share from my story for God's glory. I realize that when it's inspired by God, you know it's a journey only you are fit to travel. He gives each of His children their own measure of grace.

Becoming SUDDENLY single may sound like a sad situation according to the standards of this world. But in my case, it helped me break free from the restraints of a mentally unfit relationship. I had to endure the road, and I wouldn't wish anyone tread this path on their own.

By sharing my story, I can leave my footsteps in the dirt. It is my desire to help you experience, emphasize, and understand that although we may be different, we are quite similar.

Inner healing has been my goal. Knowing myself and placing **me** first has helped me to be free from a mental prison filled with illusions of what my love life really was.

SUDDENLY *Single*

> **Suddenly Single Moment**
> **-Your mind can free you to love or capture you in a prison of illusions.**
>
> *Safira*

***

Shortly after returning home from my second deployment, I lost my best friend, brother, and my other half: this left me broken inside. I never thought I would recover from this senseless murder and knew I would never be the same again. I was so angry because I always felt like my life should have been lost in war and his should have been spared.

My brother was murdered at a Denny's restaurant in Las Vegas where he was stabbed. The stab wounds severed his heart where he bled internally before they realized how severe his wound was.

I took on an 'I don't care attitude,' and began drinking heavily to mask my pain. This is how I coped with the loss. In addition to the loss, I was going through a bad breakup & I was six weeks pregnant and suffering a miscarriage.

When I think about a broken heart, I try to imagine if a broken one compared to the pain of a severed one.

It gave me relief to know he never suffered, but it was pain I would never wish on anyone.

I was hurt beyond what I can ever elaborate on, and I could never find the words to explain my pain. All my mind could do was picture the knife that pierced my brother's precious heart.

I am taking you down memory lane so you can understand where this hurt and broken woman saw her life unraveling. I can say this now, it all started when I gave up on myself, I forgot to love and care about myself due to depression, PTSD, and the hardship caused from my deployment. When I couple this with the loss of someone who I had spent twenty-five years of my life with, I began to go cold inside.

I forgot to feel, and I was numb without Novocain. I know the blood temperature is supposed to be warm, but mine was ice box cold.

I was scheduled to attend law school after graduating college, but again, nothing in the world mattered, because the person who I esteemed the highest was no longer with us. My brother was one of the most important people in my life. He was my breath of fresh air, so it took me months to start talking again or eating.

SUDDENLY *Single*

I started working two jobs just to keep my mind busy. I continued dealing with mental health issues stemming from my military service and my brother's untimely death. I never took days off I just went hard and took care of my daughter. I slept a few hours and went back to work. I sent my daughter home to live with my family so she could experience the southwest lifestyle. While she was away, I pulled myself together mentally, but that only drove me to work even harder.

Finally, I said to myself I am turning twenty-eight this year I am taking a few days off work to celebrate. I still question why this birthday what was so special that I needed to go hard for it. Looking back, I realized it was a part of God's plan that would impact the rest of my life.

That night I get into a bad fog, and I knew in my mind that something was going to happen. I didn't know what, but I felt it. I couldn't stop it but knew that God was preparing me for something I needed to endure. He chose me because He knew that I could handle the battle: I just had to suit up and fight. I had to go through the fiery furnace to be refined for better days.

As I am driving down a Las Vegas Street, I could see in slow motion a car coming towards me. I am thinking to myself, "Are they going to stop?"

No. They continued going straight through the red light and I am watching all this happen in slow motion.

Jan Mitchell

I repeatedly hit the brakes and to no avail my brakes would not stop.

Boom!!

I get into a tragic car accident and my entire world went black. I was outside my own flesh looking down on myself saying, "Just play the role and walk out the process. It's something you won't be able to comprehend until it's your time."

I rushed to the car that was involved in the accident and I jumped inside the sunroof because I could not get the door to open. No one on the scene could either.

I kicked the door open from the inside, while sitting in the passenger's lap holding his hand. There were two males laying crisscrossed, wearing colorful clothing & wristbands that were bright green. These types of wristbands must have been given to them at a gay nightclub they attended that night.

One was unconscious and the other was awake & confused. I immediately began rendering aid, making sure I could feel their pulse. I did not panic because there was no blood in sight.

I felt the scene begin moving in circles. You know like when the lights begin shining as if a camera crew was filming on a movie set?

SUDDENLY *Single*

I could hear the sirens but it's like they never appeared. I remember continuously repeating "Help is on the way."

Instantly my combat medic training from the military kicked in. If I kept him woke, and reassured him that everything would be ok, I was trained he would be ok. After what seemed like hours but was only eight minutes from the time I called, help finally arrived.

They begged me to get inside the ambulance. I remember screaming until they were safely inside, I wanted to make sure they were. I was fine but I didn't want to leave until I knew they were ok.

Finally, after much convincing and the paramedics saying they were ok, I relented, and ended up in the hospital. I suffered minor brain damage, a few scratches, a sore body.

I can recall being told silently "He didn't make it," after I constantly inquired about them to the nurses who were going in and out of my room. I was in utter shock and disbelief and was finally sent home.

I continued working my two jobs, when one day after work six months later I get a knock on my door. It was Metropolitan Police Department informing me I was charged with DUI death and or substantial bodily harm. Initially, I was not at fault, but the decision was later reversed.

JAN MITCHELL

I was stunned! Back into this black world I go. I went from never doing any prison or jail time in my life to now being a model inmate who every corrections officer grew to love. I finally realized that I needed to get my life back together, this ain't it.

I Prayed heavily, focused on myself, and got my sanity in order. I still didn't realize the seriousness of the disarray my life had fallen into. It was easy for me in prison because I was favored.

* * *

During my prison sentence, I met a man who I thought would complete me. He was also serving time at the same facility as myself. I would smile at him during our bus rides to work together. I would flirt, laugh and just be the happy go lucky girl I am.

If I could turn back the hands of time, I never would have flirted; but that isn't the case. From that relationship a beautiful little girl was created, so how can I really love a child if I regret whom she was created from?

Even though I could have given birth to her with a different man, why would I attempt to change God's plan? She is the gift from enduring such a frivolous relationship.

Looking back, I realized she was the only good thing that came from my troubled marriage. I can never say

I wished it had never happened because she helped me cope with the fictitious, fraudulent, conniving man I was married to. She eases the pain and embarrassment I've gone through.

I laugh because I was never hurt by the betrayal but embarrassed by how I allowed a man to misuse me. He married me for stability, a place to live, and my military benefits. How didn't I see the red flags?

> **Suddenly Single Moment**
> –Be careful of a man who moves in with you SUDDENLY. Do your homework and make sure he brings something to the table.
> —Safira

I did not see the red flags because I was still blind and broken from my past. I never healed from it because I was too busy hiding from it.

* * *

I was released from prison November 2017, when I received a phone call from him. He had been watching me on social media for the past few months and was cooking up a master plan to get his hands on my success.

He was released a year prior to my release and had gotten into another relationship. I was ok with that. I was doing my own thing and focusing on the life I planned to build upon my release from prison. I had no worries in the world: I was set.

I finally allowed him to convince me to hang out on his birthday, in April of 2018. We became friends where we hung out. He would come over to my home and cook dinner, clean, wash clothes, and **pretend** to be a man of God.

He would stalk the places I checked in at on Facebook and randomly show up. He pretended to be this nice, God fearing, educated, hardworking man who had so much to offer. The whole time, he was plotting on how he could marry me and get some of my military benefits. His plan was to stabilize his life though a woman who had her life in order but was off mentally.

He played on the fact that I was overwhelmed with my release from prison, my daughter leaving for college, and a brand I was building for myself. He wanted it all at the expense of playing all the mind games he could muster up. No trick was untried, if he could conjure it up, he would find some way to make it happen.

He would mention to me how he couldn't figure out for the life of him why I am so blessed and am able to enjoy life, travel, and receive so much love from people. He was watching and waiting on the right moments to strike, while playing the role of a supportive man, that had his woman's back, and could compliment her in whatever setting.

> **Suddenly Single Moment**
> -Be careful of the plots and plans for your life. The enemy comes to steal what you have built.
> —Safira

* * *

I had taken a trip to Alabama to attend an event where I was featured as a special guest at the end of April 2018.

Shortly after our first date, I had a moment in Atlanta, GA. On May first while returning home, I went live on Facebook and created a video that had gone viral.

Now I am dealing with the weight of the world on my shoulders. I went from being unknown to a viral sensation where media outlets, radio stations, newspapers, and even random social media people were calling nonstop. I was offered interviews and public appearances.

I said NO to all.

JAN MITCHELL

All the attention was causing me to become slightly delusional, paranoid, and suspicious. I would go places and people would recognize my voice and my jewelry, all while asking if they could get a selfie. Most people would love all the attention, but to me it's something you must be prepared for. My nefarious man would soak it all up, while telling me, it's ok. On the other hand, I would sit back and support you with whatever.

Meanwhile, my mental health was spiraling out of control because I tried to keep up with the image people loved on social media. People loved seeing us together, and he made sure when the live camera was rolling, he threw on his charm. His hopes were that I would listen to all the people who were saying, "Y'all just need to get together."

I was secretly confused, but gave in. In the back of his mind, he was silently celebrating the victory of me drawing near to him. It was him being at the right place at the right time, and his arms I chose to run into.

While I had a sense of being out of touch with reality, I was unknowingly running right into a dark trap. I was just like the mouse who got caught after longing for the shiny piece of cheese on top of the trap. As my good friend the mouse, I went right into the arms of a predator who preyed on my mental weakness.

I didn't have my mindset in order. My life was but my

SUDDENLY *Single*

mind was not. You may think, "How is that even possible?" Trust me it's possible.

I walked aimlessly into a living nightmare, while being led to believe I was living a Disney love story that would end happily ever after. I did not realize I was being taken advantage of.

I would go live on Facebook with over three hundred+ plus viewers, while soaking up the California sun. But after I hit the end button, no one felt the sadness I knew I was feeling deep down inside. I felt so incomplete, because I knew that there were red flags, but I played color blind to them.

I wanted the fairytale the world saw when I posted or went live on social media: the best looking, happy, power couple. But I knew I was trapped because I had already said, "I DO" so fast that I couldn't turn back.

On our honeymoon, I got pregnant with my baby daughter Leah. Even though we tried to get pregnant I never thought it would happen so fast. Later down the road he admitted that he tracked my ovulation to make sure that I would get pregnant. This was another one of his devised plans to ensnare me into his web of lies. I was living in the world, but my mind was far from ok. Mental health is serious especially when you are with someone who masks them with deception.

* * *

I got into a serious argument with him, and he ended up striking me and giving me a black eye. Never in my life had I allowed a man to harm me, and I let it slide. Unfortunately, the spell he cast on me was a dangerous game and I was defenseless because I'd never played the game. I was slowly finding out that I was married to a monster

He did everything he could to try and control my life. Being an intelligent woman, I wasn't going for that. I was in denial, and silently wished for it to pass. I asked God was marrying him the right decision after many nights of him taunting me and holding me down on the bed while he sat on top of me, forcing me to look into his evil grey eyes. I couldn't do anything but scream, only for my screams to go unnoticed. It's like yelling into a glass bottle, snuffed out.

> **Suddenly Single Moment**
> -Abuse in any relationship is not ok. Get out and get help. Your life is too precious to be wasted away in abuse.
> —Safira

I was embarrassed to explain to my family and friends their intuitions about him were correct, but they didn't want to share with me. I kept thinking to myself at night as I lay next to him, who am I married to? I know that I needed help, but he needed it even more.

SUDDENLY *Single*

I threatened to leave him if he didn't get help and agree to go to marriage counseling. Low and behold, when we attended counseling, he managed to fool the counselor. I knew there was something seriously wrong with this guy, and I wanted out.

He would always play the victim, and because he was Caucasian, it seemed to work. He always upgraded my mental health situation and downplayed his, getting on his knees begging me not to leave. He would admit to his dark side while giving me an evil daunting look as if to say, "You never want to see that side."

I always wanted to make it work, so I gave him chance after chance. But with all my efforts, I kept seeing, the real him: he couldn't hide it anymore. I was defrauded: I really thought my marriage was legit. But I realized I had said, "YES" to a manipulative man, who was seasoned with lies.

***

Finally, after I took my daughter to college in Alabama, I realized he was a bum, and I made the wrong choice in marrying this guy.

We had the gender reveal for my daughter and I remember this day like no other. It was the final straw, and I couldn't take it any longer.

November 2018, we got into an argument over a text I received from one of my African American brothers.

Jan Mitchell

He invited me out to lunch to talk business on Friday. I never got the chance to go out with my friend, because he called him a "Nigger" On Facebook live.

At that moment I realized I am married to a racist. This was a man whose ancestors were more than likely faithful members of the KKK, who never missed a meeting. I would tease him about it, because he admitted that his mother said he'd better not bring home a black woman. I asked him, "Well why did you do it?" His response was to 'piss her off.'

***

Less than forty-eight hours after I had the gender reveal, I was standing in front of a judge who remanded me to custody. I was four months pregnant, and accused of testing positive for THC, and I didn't smoke marijuana.

I learned later that the man who claimed to love to me and cherish me had me thrown in jail by tampering with my drug test patch that I was ordered to wear on my arm. All of this was because I threatened to divorce him.

He then said, "Yeah you won't be going anywhere with that *nigger*."

SUDDENLY *Single*

Freedom Comes In Strange Ways

After being booked into the county jail and thrown into a dirty cell, I fell to my knees and thanked God: I was finally free!!

I realized after being there for a few days, it was His plan and I had one job: walk out the process!

I blocked all his visits and didn't call him. I filed for divorce, and he went on a rampage: he was finally exposed for who he really was.

I started confessing to all my family and friends I knew the red flags were there, but I couldn't see them because they were blurred by his deceit. I couldn't imagine what my life would be like if I had not been saved by grace & taken into custody. I ended up doing thirty-two months, but I will say those thirty-two saved me.

I ended up giving birth to my beautiful baby girl shackled to a bed. No one was there holding my hand, but the nurse. The other nurse walked out and called her supervisor. She explained that she refused to work on me because she was so saddened by the fact that I had been given an epidural and they had me chained to a bed like a dog chained to a doghouse.

It was the loneliest feeling ever, but God gave me a great correctional officer who cut my umbilical cord, because I wasn't allowed any family there with me during the birthing process. I silently prayed during labor as tears flowed down my face. I was comforted by an angel who I knew came from God.

My daughter was delivered at exactly 11:11 am on 4/11.

The corrections officer stood next to me and said, "Congratulations! I watched the clock as you pushed and I prayed for you, that she would be here at 11:11. This meant the angels are attentive."

All the corrections officers who watched over me that day, said they were going to play the lottery based on the time of her birth. I was happy that she was well and healthy, she helped me through many lonely nights in that cell.

While I was pregnant, it's like she felt her mommy's struggle, but I always promised myself I would stay strong for her. I would sing gospel songs to her at night, while feeding her the oranges they gave me as a nightly snack. She would kick my belly, until she got that orange.

SUDDENLY *Single*

She was a blessing to me, because she gave me a reason to break free from the mental agony that held me captive. It was at that point that I realized it was no longer an option it was mandatory!

I got to hold my baby for forty-eight hours. It was when they rolled the wheelchair in my room and said, "Ms. Allen we are here to take you back." That was when I broke down.

It was even more heart wrenching, when they took her and I could hear her tiny voice, wailing for her mommy in the nursery. She was pushed over in a corner full of strangers' babies, and I knew at that moment, I must get this s#*! right.

It hurt me to the core of my soul! I grasped as I felt the air leave my lungs. I could hardly catch my breath because I wanted my baby and I wanted to be free. I knew I had to get well for her, it was no longer about Safira, baby Leah depended on me.

Thankfully my mother picked her up from the hospital the very next day, and she stayed with her, my sister, and stepfather until I came home. I am so blessed to have a loving family my baby could be safe with until we were reunited.

***

As I served my time in prison, I read the Bible my daughter bought me and every educational book I could find. I read a few urban books as bonuses, but during my spare reading time, I wanted to heal and elevate. I wanted to seek something that would help me to dilute my inner woman.

I read over three hundred books, while I was away. When I tell you, they changed my mind set for the best, God was in it all! I could feel the elevation of my soul, and the renewal of my mind. I loved, this new woman and couldn't wait to showcase her on a platform to the world, my family, and my friends. Not only for them but myself! Blessings were overflowing, even though I was physically locked up, I was mentally liberated.

When my daughter turned eight months old, karma reached the old shammer. He was arrested and booked for battery by strangulation on his ex-girlfriend. This was a case he was charged with before we were together. After taking her through hell, she realized his ways and kicked him out her home. He refused to leave and attacked her.

I found out the truth after we were married, but of course he had his good old playbook of lies. He turned it all on her and made it seem like she was the crazy aggressor.

* * *

When I was released in July 2021, I immediately filed for divorce which was granted and is now final. I blocked all his phone calls from prison, and he constantly wrote harassing letters, hate letters, then love letters. He filed motions to overturn the divorce, granting him alimony in the amount of fifteen hundred dollars a month, and with full custody of our child. He wrote the court begging them to send me back to prison on a parole violation because I blocked his calls and abandoned him, fraudulently divorcing him without cause.

I haven't seen him in almost three years, and I am happier than ever! I've bonded with my daughter: she ran right back into my arms as if I have never left. After my mother asked, "Do you know who that is?" I will never forget her little round face saying, "My Mommy!"

When I opened the car door. I wanted to break down and cry, but I didn't want to scare her. I just held back my tears and embraced the moment. We are now inseparable.

I took her on her first vacation by plane to Alabama. She is now officially a little traveler; she is now two months shy of turning three years old.

My oldest daughter is preparing to walk across the stage at Alabama A&M, I can't believe it's happened so fast! I am proud of her because despite my absence, she stayed the course!

JAN MITCHELL

I have been happier than ever, and I feel so safe since he has been locked up. Everyone is on pins and needles because he has an upcoming release date, mid-March.

How will we all cope with our peace being destroyed? This will be a huge test for me. I haven't given up on God, so I know He won't give up on me. But how do you deal with a man off his rocker, claiming to serve the same God you serve, all while spewing hate?

My story can't come to an end because it's yet to be lived and imagined. This version of Safira who is SUDDENLY single can't be written in full, only in sequels. This is a story I refuse to leave untold!

His release is like living a nightmare on the night of Halloween. You know when the monster is out, but you wonder what disguise will he wear to attack? I must learn to survive knowing I have an opponent, who I beat at his own game, and he isn't so happy about it.

Becoming SUDDENLY single saved my life! I conquered the mental demons; I've slaughtered them with enlightenment. I've watched them flee, and he ain't ready for this revised version of me!

I am so glad I was taken away when my mind was weak, because losing my freedom, showed me how valuable I am. I was refined by the fire, a fire that no water could quench.

I burned like a candle set on a hill alone. My soul casts a special glow and being single has helped me relocate myself. I was once lost now I am found. I was once bound now, I am free. SUDDENLY single has been a Blessing for Me!!

XXOOXX

Safira

"The poison leaves bit by bit, not all at once. Be patient. You are healing."

~Yasmin Mogahed

SUDDENLY *Single*

BECAUSE SHE'S "BLAKK"

I knew better getting in that d*$@*Blazer with Lunatic. The first clue was he gave me the keys to drive so that meant we were leaving the area. We went to get a forty alright all the way in South County to his baby mama's house.

Jennifer was of course 'white' living in South County. He visited with his son for about two hours then we made our way back to Stewart.

The sun had set and all the family members, friends and lookey loos had gone home. Now it was the repass after party on the block.

Lunatic's older brother Nine had the garage open and Patch's boat on the lawn was filled with girls drinking and dancing. When we pulled up, I could see the disappointment in Lunatics face. Instead of being his usual confrontational self, he got out and went into the house. I followed, looking around.

Jan Mitchell

It was the same old crew from Bennett's and Andersons and their inner circle. Once inside Dana the eldest daughter of the Andersons informed me Pops had went on a run and for me to wait for his return before I headed back to the IE.

After a while, I was getting agitated and being out in the garage was cold as well. I hadn't brought anything to cover my arms or a change of clothes for that matter. I walked to the boat and grabbed a black Dickie coat and asked while putting it on, "Who's coat is this?"

A few mumbles and a strong, "If you could put it on when someone starts looking for their coat, we'll know who's it is." I did just that.

I want to say about thirty minutes after I put the coat on, a little black sedan pulled on the block, tinted windows, and all. Before the car got close you could hear the music bumping. As it slowed down the music got lower.

This type of s*$! will have you with your hand on your piece ready to duck for cover. Well, me anyways.

The car gets close, and the passenger window rolls down. By this time, I have positioned myself with a few options and hopefully blasting is the last.

SUDDENLY *Single*

Suddenly, a chick from the neighborhood Kimbo pops her head out the window and says, "If y'all scared get off the block."

Everyone relaxed and came out their respective safe spots. As the greetings and bagging goes on, Slim hops out the back. She makes her way to the edge of the driveway and asks, "Marcus here?" No one replies so she starts calling individuals about where Mr. Lion was.

Then finally a dusty a*@ nigga named Cadillac answers, "Ask Blakk."

I shot him a look of disgust because he knows he's not supposed to speak my name nor look my direction. But that's ok; wait until my Pops return.

***

He got drunk one night as always, a few years back. When I was eighteen, he tried to take advantage of me one evening when I fell asleep on the couch in the Andersons' home.

My dad made a run and Lunatic, Patch and Nine were in and out. Shelly went to her sister's house for the weekend. I got tired of hanging on the corner and decided to watch 'Sanford and Son' with Mr. Anderson until he went to bed.

Jan Mitchell

I curled up in a fetal position and closed my eyes for what seemed like forever but was more like thirty to forty minutes. My sleep was interrupted by the stench of cigarettes, alcohol, and FUNK.

I opened my eyes to see Cadillac's greasy red eyed self-hovering over me. As I rubbed my eyes, I said, "What do you want? Why are you looking over me like you stupid?"

As I went to get up, he pounced down on top of me like a cat. He pinned my hands above my head and spread my legs apart all while trying to kiss on my neck and breasts.

I was squirming and wiggling, yet he continued pressing his body on me harder. The smell he carried was making me nauseous and he was dry humping me and saying you going to give me some of this pussy.

I finally got one hand free and reached under the couch pillow and grabbed my three eighty revolver and cracked him in the head with it.

He yelled, B*$!@," and punched me in my face.

By then, Mr. Anderson was calling from upstairs. He wanted everyone out and ordered us to take the horseplay outside.

I yelled out to him, "Mr. Anderson help me!"

Like clockwork, Lunatic emerged from the kitchen where he entered from the side of the house. Cadillac and I were still tussling. With no questions asked, Lunatic dropped that nigga and commenced to whooping on him until the corner boys came and pulled them apart. By then Mr. Anderson came downstairs looking around.

Lunatic said, "That nigga was supposed to be in here taking a piss. I knew s*#@ wasn't right because all of a sudden, he goes and pisses in the house like a b*$!@."

* * *

Slim looked in the direction where Dana and I were standing, fussing to her daughters about getting ready for bed.

"Tyra," she says all stank and whiny like, "Where Marcus at?"

"Why are you asking me where that nigga at? There's his car, so he's here somewhere. Why you got on my man jacket I bought him?" By this time all focus was on our conversation.

Awkwardly, I put my hands in the pockets of the jacket I had borrowed, cocked my head to the side and said "What? Who's your man?"

B*$!@, you know who my man is that's his jacket. I put those bleach spots on the sleeves.

By this time the distance between us had become smaller and all chatter was silenced. I immediately looked down at the jacket sleeves and sure enough bleach spots on the sleeve under the armpit area. So many thoughts raced around in my head and confusion set in as I thought of the moments earlier when I put the jacket on. Now the reflection of Marcus AKA Mr. Lion had worn a jacket similar unbeknownst to me, the actual jacket

In the midst of my reflecting, I hadn't noticed that Slim was now standing by my car until she started yelling, "Take it off! Where is he? They told me he was here. Take it off!" Out of nowhere, she pulled out a hammer and banged it up against my back passenger window.

So, I'm told he hid and instructed everyone that they didn't know where he was when he saw the sedan belonging to her relative hit the corner.

The relative got out of the car and was confronting her. "See that's why I don't do s*#@ for you, always out here acting a d*$@ fool over a nigga. That's why he left you alone. You were supposed to be getting money from him. You so d*$@ stupid I knew you were lying."

As she spoke people had gotten in between us and Dana was now addressing: "Slim get your little skinny ratchet a*@ from in front of my house."

"I came to get..." Slim tries to explain, but Dana cuts her off.

"Get what? Your man?" Here she nudges at Mr. Lions shoulders, "Get him and go."

I hadn't realized he was now standing in front of me until he replied, "Man girl, go on, I told you months ago we were done."

"Yeah, because you trying to come up off that ugly black *b*$!@* daddy that's all. That's the only reason why niggas talk to her tar baby a*@ anyway. She thinks she something," looking from me to my car.

"At Least she ain't ghetto and embarrassing. Go away I don't want you."

Now everyone heard it. He turned and stopped dead in my face and said, "I'll pay for your window."

As she and her folks got in the car to leave. I heard "S*#@ Blakk, couldn't have been me, I would of.."

Lunatic said, "S*#@ that little crazy *b*$!@* would have f*$#@* Blakk up with that hammer. She did right, let his buster a*@ handle his *b*$!@,* then I would have had to do both they a*@! in," laughing.

Mr. Lion remained quiet looking at me apologetically

and replied, "I got your buster nigga right here," grabbing his crouch, "She ain't my *b*$!@*."

"Well, Blakk won't be either when Killa Will find out," Nine added with a chuckle as he swept up the broken glass.

I remained silent looking around and thinking.

***

Dana came outside with her house phone and gave it to me without a word, just a smirk of sympathy. I took the phone, "Hello Tyra," his deep, raspy voice bellowed.

"Yeah Pop?"

"You cool?"

"Yea, I'm good just tripping."

"Off what? A b*$!@ tripping off you wearing her nigga jacket? That's that bull s*#@. I tell you about a nigga gone do nigga s*#@ to keep his nuts inflated. Have your own Tyra, running around here talking about you in love and you walking. Don't depend on a mother f*$#@*! to do s*#@ for you.

See her a*@ in love with no finesse about herself. What I tell you about finesse? Catching rides and s*#@ to come beg and to tear up another b*$!@ s*#@

that her man trying to f*$#@*! on. Shake that s*#@ and if I ever hear you in these streets fighting over a nigga who ain't me or your brother I'm not f*$#@*! with you no more!"

Although, I knew Will wasn't my real father I wished the words of truth he spoke were a little more nurturing and not so harshly delivered. Again, I chalked it up that he didn't know any better. He announced his self as my father to the streets and those who knew the truth never questioned it. Knowing he wasn't made to call himself my father gave me that warm feeling inside.

***

Six months had passed since the jacket incident. Pops, Lion and Lunatic had a deep discussion about it and the attraction between Lion and me. Although I'm nineteen, Lion had to reassure them he could fill their shoes with regards to my well-being and there wouldn't be any more run ins with his women counterparts.

Nonetheless, we became an item and Slim eventually fell off but not without attempting to show up a few more times. We were so on such a high making money and living life that we had decided to keep my place as the base of our operations and near the MADD house: our money maker.

Jan Mitchell

I still held my job and shared accounts with pops, but he was changing. He wanted to get a printout of all weekly deposits, so I obliged. He would call and inquire about Lion's whereabouts and if my answers weren't sufficiently conveyed, he'd always reply before ending our call with, "Niggas gone do nigga s*#@, remember that."

I thought, how couldn't I, and hung up the phone.

I went to bed for work and Lion was there sleeping. I looked at him and he felt me staring and asked, "What's up?"

I simply replied, "Nigga s*#@."

***

I arrived home to see KK, India, and another short, young, mixed girl. They were all standing at the bottom of the stairs when I reached my door.

"What's going on y'all?" just making small talk. Right away, India who is now seven months pregnant by Woody, starts in, "These two dumb mother f*$#@*! over there at the MADD house letting them niggas get high all night and Woody OD on sherm s*#@."

Puzzled, I asked, "What and who are you? KK where's Lion?"

India interjected, "All of them niggas gone. Blakk,

they took Woody to his baby momma house and guess what? She looks at KK and the girl named Candy. KK scrunches up her face at her and Candy looked down at the ground."

"What?"

India still the only one speaking and telling everything. "Especially since Woody was the center of this little controversy. This big lipped hoe and this mutt be in there all high, butt naked cooking and cleaning and doing whatever else they dumb a*!@*s to do," as she pushed her finger in KK's forehead. The funny part about it all is I felt sorry for the two girls.

India on the other hand was not fond of Candy's friendship with KK and she made sure to let KK know it. She called her dumb, a hoe and in her words you two 'yellow b*$!@s.'

"Let me find out you was sucking on Woody or Lions pee pee or anything and I'm gonna make sure she is ringing out a towel or something. Me and Blakk helped your runaway homeless a*@ and you stealing and trying to f*$#@*on her man? Uh huh I see ya, I don't be sleep I be listening to errrthang mmmhmm sure do b*$!@s."

She was so close to KK's face she could have kissed her. KK, from what I've noticed is not a confrontational person. If she's not comfortable around you, she will give you the sense that you could easily take advantage of her which happens often.

KK solemnly gave me the details of how everything went down as I wondered where Lion was at this time. Lately, I found myself questioning him about his whereabouts far more than what I'm comfortable with. Not to mention his sudden involvement with his relative Chopper who wasn't around much, maybe once or twice since the initial meeting the night of the CPT run. Those two encounters were anything less than pleasant, especially when I realized he had intentionally fed Slim information about Marcus and I the night of the jacket incident.

* * *

During the past three months a lot transpired. India gave birth to a beautiful baby girl looking like Woody. The MADD house was booming and surprisingly KK and Candy held it down. India even accepted Candys's presence to a certain degree occasionally reminding her of the history of her and KKs sisterhood.

Of everything that went on during the past months, my pops going to prison was the worst. I still think about how I drove to his house early one Monday morning after Lunatic called me expressing his concerns about him not meeting for the drop Saturday night. Not to mention Lion asked me when the last time was I spoke to my Pops.

SUDDENLY *Single*

* * *

As soon I reached my Pop's street, my stomach turned into knots. I blamed it on the coffee at first. It was the grey sedan parked backwards in front of my dad's house that caught my attention. I passed the house up made a U-turn and parked opposite on the other side of the block. I watched for movement for about fifteen minutes; nothing.

I got out the car looking for anything out of place. I go to the door and for some reason I turn the knob knowing d*@! well he always locked his door. The knob got tight and wham! The door was pulled open and there stood in grey slacks, a dark blue Polo and aviator shades: a white man.

I screamed, "Where's my pops? Who are you?" This was all while skipping backwards.

He took a couple of steps out and sarcastically asked, "Who's your pops? Are you Tyra?"

I was ready to run as I replied, "You're in his house you know who he is."

By now I was running. To where, I don't know when my car was the other direction. I got to the corner and out emerged one of my pop's women. I knew her but not like the others.

She looked scared and funny in the face. She pulled me to an area behind some shrubs where she'd been watching my pops house. We shared our concerns of him not answering calls I learned this wasn't her first time spying on my pops.

I called Lion a few times, no answer. This was his norm lately. I watched them bring out my pops and a few others and take them away. He ended up getting two years on a parole violation for a gun but no work or anything was found.

Word went around about pops, and I end up visiting him because he summoned me and not on Lion's behalf. He set me up with the connect and thanks to Unk Jam we tied up pops undone business and secured enough to keep Lion and I going.

***

Months went on and Lion disappeared. KK and Candy were hardly around; they had become a part of Choppers entourage, so I decided to give up the MADD House. This required me to clean and move things out.

One Saturday, I decided to get started. I was standing outside the window, and I heard India saying, "You better tell her before I do. Everybody talking about it, she gonna find out."

Then he spoke, "You not gonna tell her, I am. Let me hit that."

What the h*!! was Lion doing in there talking to India and did he just do drugs? I'm assuming KK and them were all there too. My chest got tight, and I returned to my apartment. I decided to stop renting the condo Lion and I shared. Money was funny plus I knew I couldn't afford it off my job salary alone.

> **Suddenly Single Moment**
> -When things appear to be off, follow your instincts and intuition.
>
> —Tyra

For the next few weeks, I stayed out of sight. Lion continued his same day to day. This particular Thursday, I received my mail and was going over my phone bill. It was thick with pages of reversed long-distance charges. I call the number with multiple entries.

"Hello, hi, I'm going over my phone bill and your number is on here a lot of times. As I'm talking, I'm looking at the time of day the calls were made. All during the times I'm working."

The voice on the other end said, "Oh really?"

"Yes. Do you know anyone in Corona? I see you're in the OC?"

"Yea, I do. Hold on."

I hear a baby cry.

The voice returns to the phone. "Hello."

I proceed to probe again, "Do you know any Bennett's?"

"Yes, I know them. I have a three-month-old baby for Marcus Bennett. Him and Chopper came to see me and my sister last night."

My body got warm and not the good warm and my heart felt like it was in my chest. I continued digging.

She asked who I was, and I tell her, "Marcus's sister Tyra."

She repeats, "Marcus' sister. Oh, hi."

I asked, "Have you talked to our mom?"

"No, only his cousins come over with him since I had the baby. Can you hold on? My other line is ringing."

A few seconds went by, and she replied, "Uh hello,

Marcus is on the other line he told me to hang up when I told him his sister was on the phone."

I asked, "Did you tell him you told me about the baby?"

She said, "Yes. He said to hang you up."

"Ok, ok. Please tell him to call me and mom."

I hang up as my legs collapsed. I was weak. I let out a cry and hugged myself crying uncontrollably. I cried for a minute then I became angry. I dialed his mama and I told her everything. She prayed the whole time.

Before we hung up, she said, "Tyra baby, don't kill him please."

I just hung up and began crying an angry cry. Then I went outside and busted out the windows on his Monte Carlo. I scratched a heart and the words your black b*$!@.

By now, India and company are outside not believing their eyes. "Blakk what happened? Stop, stop!"

I looked her dead in her eyes. "He didn't tell me she did. Now you're off the hook; free your conscience India, I know."

Jan Mitchell

I returned to my house after the numerous explanations from every one of their knowledge. I cried most of the night thinking of the betrayal and deceit until I was knocked out.

> **Suddenly Single Moment**
> **-Beware of those who hold harmful secrets.**
> *-Tyra*

As I laid on the couch, I heard him coming up the street with his music bumping. I jumped up, turned out all the lights and waited by the window.

Lion yelled, "F*@!! no she didn't man!"

Others were in shock, commenting on my work on the Monte Carlo. Here he comes...

I ran to the kitchen for a knife seeing how he took my three eighty revolver for whatever reasons.

I hear his voice get closer to the door. With my knife in hand, my heart beating fast the door opens. I pick up a glass off the sink and threw it at the door as it opened and kept throwing glasses, plates whatever made crashing noises.

SUDDENLY *Single*

It was like I got a release.

He closed the door back and called my name as I was throwing, and yelling, "Get out, get out you can't do nigga s*@! with me!"

He attempted to plead his case never closing the door.

In the background I saw India with a look of sadness. She looked at me as she stood next to him in the doorway and turned pushing him aside and closed the door as she left out.

Once outside she could be heard saying, "He deserves every bit of what she gives him."

I put him out and removed every indication he existed physically and financially. That didn't stop him from showing up unwanted, literally breaking in. I changed the locks and he'd break a window. The restraining order meant nothing to the now, 'meth head.'

Apparently, from what I've been told he started stressing out and got hooked on meth because of his guilt. I knew something wasn't right when he picked up his smoking habit.

* * *

I didn't trust him and after visiting with my pops, I scaled the operation all the way down and put my homegirl Lashae on, worked my job and ran Pops operation through them in the OC.

One Friday in May, I came home from work a little earlier than usual and I saw his Cadillac still displaying my body work parked on the street. Usually, he would be upstairs at India with Beware chilling or taking a much-needed shower.

I parked my car and scan my surroundings and hurry to my apartment. I open the door and couldn't believe my eyes. My s*@! was all I could think. My whole apartment was empty.

For about one and a half seconds I thought, I was robbed.

I walked from room to room and all my personal things were there but furniture, TVs, bar, stools, microwave, even my bedroom set was gone. Then a light bulb turned on, that nigga came in here and took my stuff.

I flew up the stairs to India's apartment who was obviously sleeping at one o'clock in the afternoon.

"Where is that nigga at?" I yelled, pushing my way in.

"Blakk who? Nobody's here but me and the baby."

"What happened now Tyra?"

SUDDENLY *Single*

"Girl that nigga took all my s*@! out of my apartment."

"D*@!*," she said, stomped her foot and sat on the couch.

Then her phone rang and it's her cousin Jbone's wife, the Wilona from the Jefferson of the family. I could tell she was talking about me by India's body language.

India hangs up and confirms she called to ask where Marcus was going with all my stuff. She saw my things on the back of the truck when he came to get Jbone for help.

I started making calls and my rounds to all his spots to let it be known I was coming for my stuff.

* * *

Monday had come and no word on my stuff yet. I went to work to organize a few accounts before I took a week off to regroup and get my mind right. When I made it home there was a note taped to my door. I grabbed it thinking it was from management. On the paper was a sentence: your stuff is at this address.

I fill India in on what I found, and she was just as shocked as I; at least that's what she wanted me to believe.

JAN MITCHELL

I went back home and call LaShae. I told her to be ready and I'd be staying a few nights as I had become fond of one of Jbone's friend over the last few months since Marcus' new baby.

LaShae and I arrived at the address and it's an apartment complex. I'm determined to wait but LaShae's man wasn't having it. He was controlling and trifling, and he had tried to hit on me.

We did not get anywhere the first night we went, so we agreed to wait. I never hid my feelings about him to her but this I would sit on.

They next night, we go back to the address and got lucky. There was the Cadillac parked on the street in a cul-de-sac. As we're getting closer, it hit me: I'll take the license plates off and make the alarm go off. He'll come out to make sure know runs off with his car.

No luck with him surfacing but a nosey neighbor called the police. I informed them about everything and that it was my car. After they ran me and the car, they advised me to tow it so I would not get into trouble.

The nosey neighbor had an earful and was excited to share all she knew. It turns out Marcus and the baby mama had moved in not too long ago. She never comes out and he's always gone with two guys in a green truck.

SUDDENLY *Single*

"Chopper," I say to LaShae.

On day three, I got an epiphany. She's on the county housing assistance, that's how they moved into that apartment. Her mother put her out when she found out she was pregnant again with Marcus's baby and the other one hadn't made a year yet.

Marcus was said to have told people he took my things because I could afford to get new stuff and half of it was his anyways. We received furniture and linens as wedding gifts from our families when they found out we had secretly gotten married in Vegas.

I decided to wait outside by the mailboxes on the first and then again, if need be, the fifteenth for her to get her check.

It worked. She came out but recognized me and ran back into the house. This time, I got to see what door she went in.

India beeps me, so I call her back. She says the girl talked to Marcus and told him what I had done, and he was on his way home. LaShae and I switched out cars and go back.

It's a few hours later and Corona was only a thirty-minute drive: he should be there by now. We walk around their building to the electrical fuse boxes, and

Jan Mitchell

I turn off all the lights to their building and waited on the steps for him to come.

Sure enough, like clockwork, the doors started opening, heads popped outdoors including Marcus. As I make my way up the stairs, he's frozen. I came inside looking for my stuff and I see my black bar stools at the door. He just kept saying my name, "Tyra, Tyra!"

By now, little Ms. $607 came up behind him yelling, "I'm calling the police."

"Call them and ask for officer Homer," I called out, "He has a report started already. See I reported my things stolen and you have all my things in there. I have proof those are my things and I want them now!"

Not really. It was just the principle.

She starts whining like a kid. I heard she just turned seventeen.

"I don't want the stuff Marcus give it back to her," She cried.

"No, no, no. Just give me a divorce and you can have it all including him," I replied.

Marcus turned to me and said, "I told you the night you put me out, one of us would die first before I let

SUDDENLY *Single*

you go," and closed the door.

* * *

A week after my standoff with Marcus and Ms. $607 I had a doctor's appointment for a sinus infection.

The doctor runs tests and labs diagnosing me with sinusitis requiring surgery. I agree to the surgery to rid me of the headaches I was having.

The doctor looks at me and says, "I'd like to schedule you Tyra, but your almost three months pregnant."

Motionless and confused I asked, "What?" and started crying.

At home, I pull myself together and called my mom. She offers support and says, "Remember I was single when I raised you."

I thought, "Wow! SUDDENLY single, pregnant, and married."

All at the same time. What a mess!

XXOOXX

Tyra

JAN MITCHELL

The Inspiration

Behind

Suddenly

Single.

ABOUT THE LEAD AUTHOR

VENUS CHANDLER

Venus is originally from Akron, Ohio, but now resides in Los Angeles, California. She is the proud mother and grandmother to three children and five grandchildren.

Her professional career spans from thirty-six dedicated years of nursing at various medical facilities. She has served at places such as Lynwood Healthcare Center, Los Angeles Community Hospital, and Bay Vista. She currently holds a Nurse Manager's position at Lighthouse Healthcare Center for the past nine years.

JAN MITCHELL

Venus is a published author, number one best-selling, international author, speaker, life coach and an advocate for survivors of childhood trauma.

In 2016, God revealed her purpose in life, which is to be an advocate for women and girls, helping them find their power, purpose, and voice. When she realized her destiny, she hit the ground running.

Since discovering her own power, purpose, and voice she can move free in the plan God has for her life.

Since then, Venus launched her own business, "Kintsugi Transformations Life Coaching Services." This organization's goal is to help women gain healthy minds. With a healthy mind we will have healthy communities. We are strength in numbers!

Having released her autobiography entitled, "A Silent Scream: My story, My Truth," she is living proof you can go after all of your dreams and achieve them one by one and everyone has purpose.

Meet The Co-Authors

Six additional Courageous women who dared to share their stories in hopes to enlighten and encourage you in your SUDDENLY Single journey.

Adrianne M. Green

Adrianne Michelle Anderson- Green aka A. Michelle is a Survivor of domestic violence. She is a victims advocate as well as an author. She recently became a podcast host for BGP and a blogger for 'Girl Boss Talk Magazine.'

Adrianne has been an employee of Los Angeles County for thirty-five years and has worked with women for over ten years, assisting them with recovering their children from the Foster Care system.

She works directly with social workers and CPS/DPSS to ensure the women she serves have completed court ordered parenting, domestic violence, and anger management classes. She has facilitated these classes and provided counseling as well.

Adrianne is very passionate about assisting women who are trying to make positive changes in their lives. She helps them do this by establishing healthy boundaries, providing skills in financial management and most importantly, identifying the red flags of abuse.

Her own story of domestic violence was written in a book called *"Stabbed to Life: The resilience of a Domestic Violence Survivor."* She wrote this book to help people understand the vicious cycle of abuse and how hard it is to get out of toxic relationships.

Being a podcast host of BGP (Big Girls Panties) another platform that promotes sisterhood and women empowerment. The platform discusses deep topics to promote discussions that educate, motivate, and inspire.

She is also a member of the Domestic Violence Coalition through Los Angeles County. This is a program designed to educate employers and the community on available resources to help people who may find themselves in domestic violence situations.

Most recently, Adrianne was asked to be a blogger with *Girl Boss Talk Magazine* and is excited to be in another position help people. She uses her own experiences as well as professional training to give good advice that can help change lives, and help people make better decisions.

She believes God allowed her to survive her brutal domestic violence attack to serve in this type of work through education and as an advocate. She understands her assignment and she fulfills it proudly with love and compassion.

You can find Adrianne on all social media platforms or reach out to her via email at: **adriannegreen@aol.com**.

SUDDENLY *Single*

Audrea V. Heard

Audrea V. Heard was born and raised in Youngstown, Ohio. September 7, 1998, marked a pivotal moment of Audrea's life. A fire erupted in her home, claiming the lives of her twenty-month-old son, and eighty-four-year-old Grandmother. Audrea was in the house, the only survivor.

Through her tragedy, Audrea began to journal her thoughts and emotions to understand this tragedy. While journaling she learned God had a purpose for her pain. In 2009 with Godly inspiration, she published her first book, "Through the Fire: Recovering the ruins of her broken life."

After writing her first book, Audrea immediately began helping other authors become published. She went on to establish the publishing company: IBG

Jan Mitchell

(Inspired By God) Publications, Inc. IBG is now a multi-faceted firm assisting authors in the areas of publishing, coaching & Marketing.

Audrea founded her personal company and brand: Audrea V. Heard Enterprises, LLC. At Audrea V. Heard Enterprises, Audrea expands her talents and abilities through books, coaching and speaking engagements.

Audrea is a Best Selling, Serial Author who has written and published 13+ books to her credit. She is passionate about what she does as an author, coach, speaker and talk show host.

Audrea resides in Jacksonville, Florida, where she runs her business full time.

You can learn more about Audrea by visiting her website: **www.audreavheard.com**.

Jan Mitchell

Jan Mitchell is a mom, certified identity trainer, and healthcare access manager.

She is co-founder and co-host of "Well, Hades!!" a Christian based internet talk show. The show is dedicated to creating a safe, non-judgmental healing space for real people to have authentic conversations.

She also currently sits on the board of directors for the National Association of Healthcare Access Management (NAHAM) as the Midwest Regional Delegate. She has also written for NAHAM's "Access Management Journal."

Kahala Adams

Pastor Kahala Adams was born in Jacksonville, Florida and is the proud mother of three children, one adopted daughter and one grandson.

She has been remarried for nineteen years to Shawn Adams.

She has obtained her BS in Communications (PR), has her Master's in Business Administration, A Master's in Christian Leadership and is currently working on her Doctorate in Theology.

She serves her community as an eighth grade Middle School teacher of Language Arts.

SUDDENLY *Single*

Safira Allen

Safira Allen is proud to be a part of the SUDDENLY Single Movement, publishing her first work of nonfiction.

She has been journaling for over twenty-five years & is an avid reader. She took a leap of faith and chose to be open about her mental relationship journey in hopes to inspire, move and educate others.

Safira was caught up in a dangerous love scandal that she must navigate to survive. Battling PTSD, she learned to maintain the mental freedom she acquired by leaving the relationship behind.

Safira is a graduate of the University of Nevada Las Vegas, where she holds a bachelor's degree in

Jan Mitchell

Criminal Justice and a Minor in Psychology. She is a veteran of the United States Army where she served overseas in the operation Iraqi Freedom War.

She holds numerous awards such as the Army Commendation Medal, Iraq Campaign Medal, and the Outstanding Volunteer Service Medal to name a few.

She is well-known across social media platforms with a large following, several viral videos in which she was given the title of "Donkey of the Day" on the Breakfast Club hosted by Charlemagne Tha God & featured on an A&E TV series titled, "Fasten Your Seatbelt," hosted by Robert Hays. She is very comical, witty & motivating and has real life content.

She was born and raised in Montgomery, Alabama but now resides in Las Vegas Nevada. She has two beautiful daughters who she cherishes with one daughter set to graduate in May 2022 from the prestigious Alabama A&M in Huntsville Alabama.

You can learn more about Safira by visiting her website: **www.safiraallen.com**.

SUDDENLY *Single*

Tyra Evans

Tyra J. Evans was born September 23, 1969. Along with her brother Val, she was raised in Santa Ana, California, by their single mother who had Tyra when she was sixteen years of age.

After watching her mother provide for her and her brother alone, Tyra had no other choice but to strive to remain at the top in everything she did.

Transportation has been most of Tyra's financial career, but she also is an entrepreneur. She obtained her business degree along with many licenses and certifications, from commercial driver, real estate, Cosmetology, notary and even a guard card.

JAN MITCHELL

In 2015 Tyra became the founder of the non-profit organization: Rydes & Beyond, Inc. She operates this business with her daughter Ta'Myra and her mother Patricia.

Over the years Tyra has made it her business to be intentional and of purpose and always encourages others to seek the same fulfillment.

Tyra's intent for sharing her life experiences is to give others hope and courage.

www.ingramcontent.com/pod-product-compliance
Lightning Source LLC
Chambersburg PA
CBHW071203160426
43196CB00011B/2187